The idea of perfect history

The idea of perfect history

*Historical erudition
and historical philosophy
in Renaissance France*

by George Huppert

University of Illinois Press

Urbana, Chicago, London

Acknowledgments

In some ways the beginnings of this book can be said to go back to as much as ten years ago, when I began my graduate studies at the University of Wisconsin. I owe more than I can say to my teachers there and at the University of California. I owe most of all to William J. Bouwsma, who directed my doctoral dissertation at Berkeley and who has remained, ever since, an indispensable and charitable critic and friend.

Among my colleagues and masters I wish to single out those who, in the last several years, have been most generous with their advice: Hans Baron of the Newberry Library, whose suggestions shaped the course of my inquiry several times; Donald Kelley of the State University of New York at Binghampton, whose erudition and generosity have helped me avoid many mistakes over the years; George Nadel and Richard Vann of *History and Theory,* whose sharp criticism whipped portions of the book into shape; Fernand Braudel of the Collège de France, whose wisdom I learned to depend on; my fellow members of the University of Chicago Seminar on the Renaissance, whose formidable collective erudition was brought to bear on portions of the manuscript at an early stage; and, finally, my friend and colleague John B. Wolf, who went over the entire book twice and can be said, in fact, to have edited it. I need hardly add that while this book benefited immensely from the suggestions of my colleagues, masters, and friends, its shortcomings are to be attributed to the author alone.

I gratefully acknowledge aid of a more tangible form: from the Woodrow Wilson Foundation (1958–1959), which made it possible for me to pursue my studies in graduate school; the Social Science Research Council (1961–1962), which gave me the opportunity of working in French libraries; the American Council of Learned Societies which, through the grant of a fellowship (1965–1966), made the research for this book possible; and the generous aid provided over the years by the research boards and committees of the California State College at Hayward and the University of Illinois at Chicago Circle.

I gratefully acknowledge the help given me, in particular, by the librarians of the Bibliothèque Nationale in Paris and of the Newberry Library in Chicago. Finally, to my wife, Loretta, I owe most of all: among other things, she is specifically responsible for much of the research which went into Appendix I.

Chicago, September, 1969

Contents

Note on translations and quotations

The rule followed here may not appear entirely clear or consistent at first glance. It is, in reality, quite simple. Quotations in another language—most commonly French—are usually translated in the text. If the quotation is a very important one and subject to more than one interpretation, the original has been added in parentheses in the text. Usually the original is relegated to a footnote. Occasionally, in the case of short phrases whose meaning in the context is quite clear to any reader, there has been no need to translate. The goal throughout has been to make the evidence easily accessible to the nonspecialist reader.

The idea of perfect history

Introduction

First chapter

The modern mind is an historical mind. We make immense efforts to perceive the past clearly: we maintain thousands of professional historians; history is taught in every school; and historical societies exist everywhere. No portion of our lives is exempt from this historicizing: church history, the history of art and architecture, and the history of science are examples of the pervasive presence of the historical spirit.

It is not so much that we worship the past for its own sake. When we visit a museum or when we travel to ancient places, we may not always commune in spirit with the dead, but we require that the statues and palaces be assigned a definite place in some tidy scheme. We want to know the date of the object's creation and the maker's name, if nothing else. Schoolchildren must memorize the dates of successive reigns as if this gave them some hold on the past.

Now this historical coloring of our mentality is unusual; together with the growth of the sciences, it distinguishes our civilization from all previous ones. Yet we know very little— almost nothing—of the origins of our historical-mindedness. Admittedly, this is a diffuse and complicated subject. To trace the history of a sentiment is no easy task, but even if we restrict ourselves to the study of the origins of history as a formal discipline, we do not get very far. Can we answer the question: did historiography begin with Herodotus or was historical science as we understand it born in the Berlin seminars of the nineteenth century?

If we work backwards from Ranke's generation to Gibbon's, we can establish some few things. The method of the nineteenth-century historians owes much, clearly, to the erudition of eighteenth-century university professors.[1] We do not always know where they themselves learned their trade and we cannot assert that their erudition was fundamentally different from or superior to that of their seventeenth-century predecessors.[2] We do not know whether the scholarship of the seventeenth-century historians and antiquarians amounted to a definite progress over the work of the late humanist *érudits* of the sixteenth century. Where, then, does modern historiography begin? What are its fundamental presuppositions, its distinguishing marks? Did historiography, as a learned discipline,

[1] See Herbert Butterfield, *Man on His Past* (Cambridge, Mass., 1955).

[2] Although the recent work of Andreas Kraus, *Vernunft und Geschichte, die Bedeutung der deutschen Akademien für die Entwicklung der Geschichtswissenschaft im späten 18 Jahrhundert* (Freiburg, Basel, Vienna, 1963), is a good beginning.

progress? From what beginning? At what speed? Was its progression retarded? Under what circumstances?

The surest guide to this entire question of the origins of modern historiography is Professor A. D. Momigliano, who starts with the assumption that "the whole modern method of historical research is founded upon the distinction between original and derivative authorities."[3] He tries to discover when and how this distinction came into being. This necessarily leads him to an investigation of the history of antiquarian studies in the sixteenth, seventeenth, and eighteenth centuries, and from there to his main theme, which is the story of the coming together of the methods of antiquarian research and the method of the general historian.

This is a most important story. For it seems clear that historical research was practiced for centuries without seriously affecting the writing of histories. The two activities were kept separate, even on occasion in the mind of a single man. Modern historiography is not the result of the discovery of historical criticism. That discovery had been made much earlier. What did change in the late eighteenth century was the climate of opinion which, all at once, made it necessary for historians to avail themselves of the researches of antiquarians or to become antiquarians themselves. In short, history ceased to be literature and became a science. Just when and for what reasons this change occurred is one of the main topics in the history of historiography. This book is a contribution to this topic.

My strategy leads straight to the French Renaissance. The tradition of humanist learning, an Italian monopoly in the

---

[3] In his article "Ancient History and the Antiquarian," *Journal of the Warburg and Courtauld Institutes* 13 (1950), pp. 285–315. This all-important essay was published again in Momigliano, *Contributo alla storia degli studi classici,* 2 vols. (Rome, 1955). All the articles referred to in this paragraph can be found in the two volumes of *Contributi,* the second of which was published in Rome in 1960. Some of the essays from *Contributi* were republished in a handy American paperback edition: Momigliano, *Studies in Historiography* (New York, 1966).

fifteenth century, had become the common property of Europeans around 1500. In the course of the sixteenth century the leadership in classical studies was moving from Italy to France, where the religious controversies which were putting such heavy restraints on academic freedom everywhere else in Europe were felt less sharply. There one could still speak "a l'academique." As late as 1534, after all, the king himself had not quite decided whether he ought to discourage the new doctrine, and throughout the sixteenth century a great number of French intellectuals—officially Catholic or Reformed—held views which escaped classification: they were libertines in both the Calvinist and the Jesuit vocabularies. In the latter half of the century the struggle between the crown, the Catholic League, and the Huguenot leadership prevented the creation of a monolithic doctrinal establishment. The Edict of Nantes was the product of this fragile equilibrium: toleration from necessity.

The weakness of divided officialdom made thought-control ineffective in France, especially since the intellectuals—*les doctes*—formed a close-knit, wealthy, and powerful group. Most of them were *gens de robe longue*, new men, trained in the law, whose family roots were firmly established in the bourgeoisies of provincial cities. Their fathers were mayors and city council men; their brothers were royal officers and administrators in towns like Sens, Provins, Beauvais, and Troyes. Other members of their families had studied theology and added clerical benefices to the family fortunes. Still others practiced medicine, taught at provincial universities, or were *notaires*. Some had married into the older nobility. However, the highest goal of the *bourgeoisie de robe*, the climax of their careers and of their fortunes, was membership in one of the *parlements*, the sovereign law courts.

It was among these *parlementaires*, many of whom had made it to the top of the social pyramid only recently, that French culture in the sixteenth century found its social setting. One need only consult the *Who's Who* of this world, François de

La Croix du Maine's *Bibliothèque françoise* (Paris, 1584), to be stunned by the preponderance of *robins* among the writers, artists, philosophers, historians, scientists, physicians, and other intellectuals in France (see Appendix I).

The *robin* intellectuals' most serious and most original contribution to historiography lay in their antiquarian researches, in their collecting and editing of medieval sources, in their histories of French institutions. At court, in the literary and scientific *salons*, in academic chairs, and in the chambers of the *parlements* and *chambres des comptes*—where classical scholarship was the key which could open all doors—in this mandarin world of the French humanists, historical erudition flourished in a great burst of well-publicized activity.

The science of chronology and the art of editing were perfected under the aegis of flamboyant virtuosi like J. J. Scaliger. The method of the philologists was applied not only to the literature of antiquity but also, and with great success, to the records of the medieval period. The study of feudal law was pursued side by side with that of Roman law. Medieval *coutumes* were collected and published. Large enterprises, such as the publication of a *corpus* of the medieval sources for French history, were begun. In general, by 1600 a solid basis had been created for the progress of historical studies.

This "French Prelude to Modern Historiography" has not escaped the attention of modern scholars.[4] Over fifty years ago, Friedrich von Bezold drew attention to its existence and to its importance for the history of historiography.[5] He suggested that one could speak of a genuine "historical movement" associated with the Parisian *parlement*, cited the names of many of its leaders (Jean Bodin, François Baudouin, Loys Le Roy, François Hotman, Jean Du Tillet, Estienne Pasquier, Pierre

[4] The best brief introduction to the topic is the chapter "The French Prelude to Modern Historiography" in J. G. A. Pocock, *The Ancient Constitution and the Feudal Law* (Cambridge, 1957).

[5] Friedrich von Bezold, "Zur Entstehungsgeschichte der historischen Methodik," *Aus Mittelalter und Renaissance* (Berlin, 1918); first published in *Internationale Monatschrift* 8 (1914).

Pithou, Claude Fauchet, René Choppin, Guy Coquille), and pointed to some of the chief problems worth investigating in this connection: the nationalism of these office-holding *bourgeois* during the political crisis of the civil wars; their Protestant sympathies; the skeptic attacks on historical method; and the connection between jurisprudence and historical erudition.[6]

The questions raised by Bezold about the evolution of historical method in the context of late Renaissance humanism as well as the broader questions about the relationship between erudition and historiography raised by Momigliano have served as the scaffolding for this study. Broadly speaking, the purpose of this book is to place the French historical movement of the sixteenth century in the general context of the growth of historical science.

An important qualification must be made at this point. The histories chosen here as representative of a particular trend in

---

[6] Since 1918 a number of special studies have appeared. From the literature on Bodin I should select the following two monographs as especially aimed at Bodin as philosopher of history: John L. Brown, *The "Methodus ad facilem historiarum cognitionem" of Jean Bodin: A Critical Study* (Washington, D.C., 1939); and Julian H. Franklin, *Jean Bodin and the Sixteenth Century Revolution in the Methodology of Law and History* (New York, 1963). There are good book-length studies of Fauchet by J. Espiner-Scott, *Claude Fauchet* (Paris, 1938), and of Masson by Pierre Ronzy, *Papire Masson, un humaniste italianisant* (Paris, 1924). There is a recent article on La Popelinière by Myriam Yardeni, "La conception de l'histoire dans l'oeuvre de La Popelinière," *Revue d'histoire moderne et contemporaine* 11 (1964), pp. 109–126, and two essays on special aspects of La Popelinière's work: Corrado Vivanti, "Le scoperte geografiche e gli scritti di Henri de La Popelinière," *Rivista storica italiana* 74 (1962), pp. 1–25, and George Wylie Sypher, "La Popelinière's Histoire de France," *Journal of the History of Ideas* 24 (1963), pp. 41–54. There is the essay on Pasquier by Paul Bouteiller, "Un historien du XVIᵉ siècle: E. Pasquier," *Bibliothèque d'humanisme et Renaissance* (1945), pp. 357–392, and the dissertation by Robert Bütler, *Nationales und universales Denken im Werke E. Pasquiers* (Basel, 1948). There is a biographical essay by Louis de Rosanbo, "Pierre Pithou," *Revue du XVIᵉ siècle* 15 (1929), pp. 279–305. There is an erudite essay on François Baudouin by Donald R. Kelley, "Historia Integra: François Baudouin and His Conception of History," *Journal of the History of Ideas* 25 (1964), pp. 35–57. There are also essays on Du Moulin by Kelley, "Fides Historiae," *Traditio* 22 (1966), pp. 347–402; and on Budé by Kelley, "Budé and the First Historical School of Law," *American Historical Review* 72 (1967), pp. 807–834.

Renaissance historiography have this in common: they all deal with the distant past. There was, of course, a large body of historical literature concerned with chronicling contemporary events. Some of these contemporary histories, from Phillipe de Commines' *Memoirs* to J. A. de Thou's *History of His Time*, were among the most widely read, most appreciated, and most influential historical works of the time. However, the chief technical and philosophical difficulties which face the historian of the past simply do not exist for the historian of the present, who has his own difficulties to contend with. For this reason, the writers of contemporary history are not considered in this study.

That there were antiquarians, erudite and technically proficient collectors of facts about the past, has, of course, always been clear; but to what extent can erudition be said to have been successfully applied to historical problems in the sixteenth century? That is the topic of the first part of this book (Chapters 2, 3, and 4). Here I show that erudition did conquer historiography before 1600 but that the conquest did not prove to be permanent. The researches of sixteenth-century scholars were often rejected by later generations of historians on obscurantist grounds. This explains what misled us into thinking of critical historiography as a late development.

In the second part (Chapters 5, 6, 7, and 8) I turn my attention to "the varied attempts to make a scientific use of historical data."[7] Here I try to show how closely the progress of erudition is connected with the philosophy of history. By studying the chief theorists of the "New History,"[8] from Jean Bodin

[7] These topics and categories, indeed the entire plan of this book, I owe to practical suggestions in Butterfield, *Man on His Past*.

[8] The phrase "New History" is used by La Popelinière in the title of his *Dessein de l'histoire nouvelle des françois* [Project for a New History of the French] (Paris, 1599). The idea that a new kind of history was in the making and that they were its artisans—new not only as opposed to the medieval chronicles but also new when compared to the histories of the Ancients; in short, altogether new—is clearly stated in all the works studied in this book, especially in the prefaces and introductions of the works of Pasquier, Bodin, Vignier, and La Popelinière.

to Henri La Popelinière, I hope to make clear that the critical treatment of sources carried with it the destruction of previously held generalizations about the course of human history. At the same time, men felt the need for a new construction to be put on the new data. From Bodin to La Popelinière this construction grew, and acquired the shape of an imagined "perfect history" whose subject was the story of the rise of civilization. This *histoire accomplie* turns out to be, in my estimation, nothing less than the matrix from which many later ideas about the meaning of history, including our own, are descended.

History should be general. It should encompass all past civilizations when the records make this possible. History is the story of human progress, of liberty, and of the rise of nations. No human activity should, in principle, be foreign to the historian —including economic and cultural activities. These ideas about history, familiar to us since the eighteenth century, are, in fact, already the mainstays of the sixteenth-century theorists.

Even our preferences in the matter of dividing up the past into epochs, ages, and periods are identical with the choices made by the sixteenth-century historians in their more pedagogical moments. To what extent there is a direct link between this sixteenth-century philosophy of history and the later, more familiar, ideas of the eighteenth- and nineteenth-century historians, I cannot say. This will have to wait for new probes into the obscure territory of clandestine culture in seventeenth-century France.

The topic of the ninth chapter is the existence of historical-mindedness in the sixteenth century. Here I proceed with some of the questions raised by Friedrich Meinecke in mind and show that both the "developmental concepts" (*Entwicklungsbegriffe*) and the "individualizing approach" (*individualisierende Denkweise*), whose combination Meinecke described as the essence of historicism, were pervasively present in the thought of the "New Historians."[9] Here again, I confess that the connec-

[9] See Friedrich Meinecke, *Die Entstehung des Historismus* (Berlin, 1936), Chap. 2.

tions between the sixteenth-century movement and later manifestations of these attitudes are not entirely clear to me. In any case, putting the spotlight on the French section of the Republic of Letters so early in its history can only result in illuminating a great many obscurities concerning the connections between Renaissance humanism and the Enlightenment.

As I hope to make clear in the next chapter, this New History proclaimed by the theorists Bodin and La Popelinière, and of which Pasquier and Vignier were the most successful practitioners, was not—and could not be—something entirely new under the sun. These scholars owed and often acknowledged enormous debts to the erudite antiquarians, to the jurists, and to the writers of political and ecclesiastical history who preceded them, especially in Italy. My concentration on the achievements of the Parisian circle is not meant to diminish the importance of earlier erudition, and I do not mean to imply that only in France was significant progress made in the techniques of erudition in the late sixteenth century. The contribution of the Frenchmen may eventually come to be seen as only part of a trend present throughout Europe.

Rather than write a series of full-scale monographs on each of the historians, I chose to give a briefer treatment in each case. This has made it possible to tie a great many loose strands together. To be sure, this account falls far short of providing a synthesis. Perhaps it even falls short of some minimum standard of cohesiveness. For this I beg the reader's indulgence. Had I seriously attempted to settle the issue at the very moment of bringing it to his notice, I would have been guilty of uncommon presumptuousness. It is my hope, therefore, that the reader will settle for something less than definitiveness and accept this as an argumentative book.

The old histories
and
the new historians

Second chapter

Frech historical writing in the early sixteenth century, if one excludes the memoirs, commentaries, and other genres of contemporary history, seems to fall naturally into one of two main traditions: it belongs either to the medieval tradition of the universal chronicle, or to the newer Italian tradition of patriotic histories written in imitation of the Roman historians. Nicole Gilles' *Annales* are a good example of a history in the first of these traditions.[1] These *Annales* begin with the Creation

[1] Nicole Gilles, *Les tres elegantes, tres veridiques et copieuses annales des tres*

and follow the traditional Christian division of human history into seven ages: the first age begins with Adam, the second with Noah, the third with Abraham, the fourth with David, the fifth with the Babylonian Captivity, the sixth with the coming of Christ, and the seventh age, still in the future, will begin with the Last Judgment and will last eternally in Heaven. But these old trappings do not mean much to Gilles. He is in a hurry to come right down to the specific subject of his history: the kings of France.

Legends and miracles abound in his book. The Roman empire is still standing. Giants are as common as kings—and, like kings, they pride themselves on their ancestry: the giant Ferragut whom Count Roland slays in Spain, for instance, is a descendant of Goliath. The walls of fortresses crumble through the intercession of saints, and the kings of France seem to have a special affinity with talking birds: Charlemagne, in the course of a crusade he undertook to conquer Jerusalem, loses his way in the woods and is rescued by a bird which talks to him and guides him safely to Jerusalem.

Gilles' *Annales* could not tell his readers much about the past. They must, all the same, have fulfilled some needs, judging from their publishing history. If one considers those "elegant, truthful and copious annals" as imaginative literature, then most of their shortcomings become irrelevant. The epic stories of Roland, of Charlemagne, and of Francio, the Trojan founder of the Frankish monarchy, had a great appeal in the days of Francis I. These stories exalted the chivalric virtues of glorious ancestors and there was no lack of interesting deeds and edifying miracles in them. No amount of sophistication and intellectual culture could prevent the enjoyment of these attractive legends of the national past. The distinction between

---

preux, tres nobles, tres chrestiens et tres excellens moderateurs des belliqueuses Gaules . . . (Paris, 1525). Gilles was secretary to Louis XII. He died in Paris in 1503. His *Annales* first appeared in Paris in 1492; its popularity is attested to by the number of successive editions: 1525, 1527, 1536, 1538, 1541–44, 1547, 1551, 1553, 1562–66, 1571, 1573, 1585, 1617, and 1621.

history and epic fiction was not clearly recognized at court.[2]

Besides being a depository of epic literature, the histories written in the medieval tradition served a philosophical function. The universal and providential character of these histories still provided for the sixteenth-century reader a fundamental bond between the past, the present, and the future—a bond which had become indispensable after a thousand years of Christian civilization. Gilles' *Annales* and other old-fashioned chronicles of this kind remained popular throughout the century, and their popularity was not at all restricted to an uneducated public.[3]

However, in the last years of the fifteenth century, when Gilles was compiling his annals in the spirit of a very old tradition, Paris and the court of Louis XII were not unaffected by new ideas. Under the guidance of Guillaume Fichet, a professor at the Sorbonne, a printing press was installed at the university in 1470 and around Fichet a circle formed, a small academy where Petrarch and the Roman poets were read. After Fichet's departure for Rome in 1471, the acknowledged leader of this circle was Robert Gaguin, who in 1473 became the General of the Order of Trinitarians and ten years later dean of the *faculté du décret* at the university. Gaguin made several journeys to Italy, and in Paris he was the friend, teacher, or patron of some of the best minds of his day, including Erasmus, Beatus Rhenanus, Reuchlin, and Budé.[4] In 1495 he published a *Compendium* of French history. In the preface to this new historical composition Gaguin announced his intention of breaking with the tradition of the old chroniclers, but the novelty he claimed for his work was one of style only. He saw his work as a process

2 See, for example, Guillaume du Bellay, *Epitomé de l'antiquité des Gaules et de France* (Paris, 1556).

3 See W. Kaegi, *Chronica Mundi* (Einsiedeln, 1954), p. 43, and Espiner-Scott, *Fauchet,* p. 283.

4 A. Renaudet, *Préréforme et humanisme à Paris (1494–1517)* (Paris, 1916), pp. 83, 116.

of "pruning" in order to fit the "verbose compilations" of his predecessors into the "solemn elegance of historical style."[5] In this he announced a new direction for French historiography at the turn of the century.

This new direction is much more apparent in the history of France composed by Gaguin's rival, Paolo Emilio of Verona.[6] The French monk had found fault with the medieval chronicles only insofar as their literary composition lacked the order and charm he admired in the ancient Roman and modern Italian histories. The Veronese *littérateur* objected to the chronicles not only on stylistic grounds but, in a far wider sense, he was contemptuous of them as barbarous and untrustworthy creations of a dark age. For Emilio, as for his Italian predecessors and contemporaries who wrote history in the tradition established by Leonardo Bruni, the poverty of the medieval chronicles could be measured by the extent of their divergence from classical standards of historical writing.[7] The preoccupation of the medieval writers with miracles and saints and their insistence on finding evidence of divine intercession in most historical events meant little to the Italian humanists; to them history was past politics. While the chroniclers understood history as the praise of God, Petrarch had asked "What else then is all history, if not the praise of Rome?"[8] Emilio brought these humanist views to his new task. He patterned his history after

[5] On Gaguin see especially Katharine Davies, "Late XVth Century French Historiography as Exemplified in the *Compendium* of Robert Gaguin and the *De Rebus Gestis* of Paulus Aemilius" (Ph.D. diss., University of Edinburgh, 1954).

[6] Paolo Emilio, *De rebus gestis Francorum libri IIII* (Paris, 1517). On Emilio see Davies, "Late XVth Century French Historiography."

[7] On Bruni's historiographical principles see W. K. Ferguson, *The Renaissance in Historical Thought* (Cambridge, Mass., 1948), pp. 3–11; H. Baron, "Das Erwachen des historischen Denkens im Humanismus des Quattrocento," *Historische Zeitschrift* 147 (1932), pp. 5–20; B. L. Ullman, "L. Bruni and Humanistic Historiography," *Medievalia et Humanistica* 4 (1946), pp. 45–61.

[8] T. E. Mommsen, "Petrarch on the Dark Ages," in *Medieval and Renaissance Studies* (Ithaca, N.Y., 1959), p. 122.

Roman models and chose from his medieval sources mostly the kind of material suitable for political history. Much of the miraculous and legendary matter of the chronicles was thus excluded from his history, but the new history which emerged from his labors was not more solidly founded in fact than the chroniclers' naïve fables had been. Charlemagne's conquest of Pamplona, for example, is a set piece narrative for both the medieval chronicler and the humanist historian. In Gilles' *Annales* the story begins in the middle of the night in the royal garden where Charlemagne, who has trouble sleeping, has a vision. St. James (*le glorieux baron monseigneur sainct Jacques cousin germain & apostre de Jesus Christ*) appears to him. After giving the king his proper genealogical credentials (cousin of Jesus Christ, brother of St. John the Baptist, etc.), the saint comes to the point: what is bothering him is that his mortal remains lie in Spain which is in the hands of the Saracens. He demands that Charles conquer the territory. This brings Charles and his army to the walls of Pamplona, but the walls turn out to be impregnable. After months of trying, the Christian army gives up, and Charles asks for the saint's help. St. James obliges, the walls crumble miraculously, and the Christians ride in, joyfully butchering the infidels.

Now, in Emilio's version there is no saint and there are no miracles. The reader is wrenched away from the personalities of medieval epic and romance into an entirely different world, that of Roman military campaigns. In the terse prose of a Roman general, Emilio gives a businesslike and, of course, entirely imaginary account of the siege of Pamplona. Charlemagne addresses his officers in the best classical manner; he concerns himself, as a good commander should, with the smallest details of camp security: trenches are dug, sorties made by the garrison, and assault is given. At last, having entered the city— not through the intercession of a saint but through Charlemagne's Roman generalship—we are about to witness the same happy ending as in the chronicle, that is, the massacre of the infidels. But no; at the last moment, Charlemagne, with true

Roman *humanitas*, spares the Saracens.[9] The description of the siege was useful to Emilio as a means of emphasizing the military merits of Charlemagne. To the medieval chroniclers the siege offered an opportunity to emphasize the religious merits of the emperor. Neither knew what actually happened, and neither cared very much.

Emilio's history is quite outside the medieval tradition, but it is not, on the whole, distinguished from that tradition by its critical method. The novelty of Emilio's history lies in its focus on political events and in its coherent narrative in which one event follows reasonably from another. These qualities assured his success. His history was published in several editions and in translation and "continuations" throughout the sixteenth century.[10] The book served as the model of Bernard de Girard Du Haillan's *History of France* and through Du Haillan, Emilio's stately prose and vivid imagination were transmitted to François Mézeray.[11] Thus the fancies of the medieval writers were replaced by new fancies. Indeed, the very plausibility of Emilio's history may have retarded the development of a critical historical tradition in France.[12]

Neither the medieval tradition nor Emilio's rhetoric could give much satisfaction to those who seriously set about the task of studying the history of France in the 1540s and 1550s.

[9] Gilles, *Annales* (Paris, 1544), f. 52rv; Emilio, *De rebus gestis Francorum* (Paris, 1517), f. LIIIv–f. LVIr.

[10] The first complete edition of Emilio's history, *De rebus gestis Francorum libri X* (Paris, 1539), was also published in 1544, 1548, 1550, and 1555. In 1565 a new edition appeared which included a continuation which brought it up to date. This edition was published again in 1569, 1577, and 1601. French translations appeared in 1556 and 1581. Emilio's book crowded Gaguin's *Compendium* off the publishing lists. Gaguin's history (1497, 1500, 1511, 1521, and 1528) disappeared in its original form, but it began a new career in a French version, *La mer des chroniques*.

[11] Emilio's talented description of the soldiers' feelings as they crossed the Pyrenees on the way to conquer Pamplona, for instance, is found repeated in Bernard de Girard Du Haillan, *Histoire generale des roys de France* (Paris, 1615), I, p. 145, and in François Mézeray, *Histoire de France avant Clovis* (Paris, 1643), I, p. 172.

[12] Ronzy makes this case in *Masson*, p. 231.

Such men were almost without exception the sons of gentlemen and magistrates who were destined to follow their fathers' careers in the law courts and in the service of the royal administration. Their education and their professional training made it difficult for them to appreciate either Gilles' or Emilio's productions. Typically they had learned Latin and Greek—sometimes even Hebrew—before they went off to the Parisian colleges for their formal education. Pierre Pithou, for example, seems to have learned all three languages, at least in an elementary fashion, in his father's house in Troyes before going on to the *Collège Boncourt* in Paris where he continued his studies under the direction of one of the best known classical scholars of the time, Adrien Turnèbe. There he probably met La Popelinière, who was two years his junior and also studied under Turnèbe.[13] A similar early grounding in the classical languages was the natural lot of other boys from *robin* families. Montaigne was just such a boy.

After this early and thorough study of the Latin and Greek languages,[14] the young scholars were introduced to the literature of the ancient world. Here, very early, their interest in history must have been born not only through their reading of the ancient historians but through the essentially historical nature of their studies. To apprehend the beauty of Latin prose and the special character of Roman morality; to understand, later, the nature of Roman law; to live so much of the time through the imagination in a world different from one's own;

[13] On Pithou see the article in Haag, *La France protestante*, and Louis de Rosanbo's casual notice, "Pierre Pithou érudit," *Revue du XVIe siècle* 16 (1929), pp. 301–330. On La Popelinière (1540–1608), see Chap. 8 *post*; on Turnèbe's role in his education, see Henri La Popelinière, *Idée de l'histoire accomplie* (Paris, 1599), p. 259. Pasquier studied at the Collège de Presles, where Ramus may have taught him (D. Thickett, *Pasquier: choix de lettres* (Geneva, 1956), p. vii). Jean Bodin, too, may have studied under Turnèbe (J. Moreau-Reibel, *J. Bodin et le droit public comparé* (Paris, 1933), p. 5).

[14] As an example of the thoroughness of their classical studies see Claude Fauchet's habit of taking notes in Greek and Latin (Espiner-Scott, *Fauchet*, p. 288).

these aspects of a humanist education in Renaissance France compelled an historical outlook. There is nothing surprising in La Popelinière's statement to the effect that he had devoted himself to history since his youth, apparently against the will of his parents.[15] This interest in history, at least among the well-to-do and educated, can be taken as one of the marked characteristics of the age. Not until the Romantic era was history to enjoy such favor in France again.

The enthusiasm for history as *magistra vitae* had taken the form, earlier in the century, of an almost naïve and seemingly insatiable curiosity concerning the Ancients. One wished to know all aspects of their way of life in the greatest detail.[16] These preoccupations informed the work of Guillaume Budé and the philologists and antiquarians of his generation. This thirst for a knowledge of the ancient world made the fortunes of teachers of Latin and Greek, and it lay behind the immense success of the translations of ancient works of literature.

By the middle of the century, however, this antiquarian curiosity began to reveal itself under a somewhat different guise. Already in Budé's work, which exerted a profound influence among the learned, one can see motives at work which do not proceed entirely from an antiquarian interest in the ancient past.[17] The entire world of French humanism tended to infuse its understanding of the Ancients with patriotic French motives. At first it may have been only a question of refuting Italian claims, of showing, as Budé did, that the French were as capable of humanistic studies as the Italians. Indeed, beyond the dispute with the Italians, another, far more purposeful quarrel was dawning, the quarrel of the Ancients and the Moderns.

"What? Shall we bear the name of Frenchmen, that is to say franc and free, and nevertheless subject our minds to a foreign

---

[15] La Popelinière, *Dessein,* p. 332.

[16] Louis Delaruelle, *Guillaume Budé* (Paris, 1907), p. 131.

[17] See Kelley, "Budé."

tongue!" exclaimed one of the younger scholars in a letter addressed to the master classicist, Turnèbe.[18] Another claimed that there was no good reason to believe in the intrinsic superiority of the ancient writers. For historians, the history of the modern nations was at least as challenging and fruitful a subject as the history of Rome or Greece; it was only for lack of talented historians that the French had not as yet produced histories to compare with those of Tacitus or Polybius.[19] Another of these young men, also a student of Turnèbe's, claimed to see around him such a profusion of new talent that he expected very soon to see histories of France written which would surpass the most famous ancient histories in every respect.[20]

Despite these high expectations, the fact remained that the existing histories of France could not stand comparison with the classical histories. The medieval chroniclers, as Fauchet put it, "failed in the chief responsibility of the historian, which is telling the truth."[21] La Popelinière observed that the chief failing of French historical writing was that "no man of honor ever practiced it since the profession had always been in the hands of clerics."[22] Pithou also blamed the deficiencies of French historical writing on the monopoly the clergy had exercised over its practice. In his view, the clergy were incapable of fulfilling the proper role of historians, since their peculiar

[18] Estienne Pasquier in a letter written in 1552, in *Oeuvres* (Amsterdam, 1723), II, p. 3.

[19] Jean de Serres, a colleague, contemporary, and correspondent of Pasquier, in his *Inventaire général de l'histoire de France* (Paris, 1624), I, 32. On De Serres (1540–1598), see C. Dardier, "J. de Serres, historiographe du roi," *Revue historique* 22, 23 (1883), and G. Huppert, "Four Modern Historians of the French Renaissance" (M.A. thesis, University of Wisconsin, 1959).

[20] "Ie voy ce iourd'huy des esprits si nets et entiers, des iugemens si universels, (chose rare aux plus excellentes Republiques qui furent oncques). Parmi ceste tant rare troupe, plusieurs se façonnans au Modelle d'un vray Historiographe: me font esperer de voir en brief l'Histoire de nostre France devancer en toute sorte de merite la plus renommée de toutes celles que nous ont laissé les Grecs et Latins." La Popelinière, in the preface to *La vraye et entiere histoire des troubles* (La Rochelle, 1573).

[21] Espiner-Scott, *Fauchet*, p. 283.

[22] La Popelinière, *Dessein*, p. 343.

limitations and prejudices stood in the way of an objective appraisal of worldly events.[23]

They turned from the chronicles to the humanist tradition of historical writing and found much to admire there. In the histories of the Italians the young Frenchmen found an approach to the past which corresponded to many of their own aspirations. The humanists taught the importance and usefulness of history as the key to the difficulties of the present. And this was more than a mere echo of the Roman writers who saw history as "the eternal treasury of examples, the living image of human life, always applicable in all times, the book of kings and magistrates, the teacher of life, the link with Antiquity, the life of memory, the light of truth, the witness of time."[24]

The vogue of history among the humanists was only in part due to the opinions of Cicero. There were deep motives within Renaissance culture for the elevation of history from romance and memoir to the level of a social science, of "certissima philosophia."[25] The modern Italian historians made of history a vast reservoir of political precedents from which present and future statesmen could learn to act wisely. The princes and generals who inhabit the Italian histories are understandable human beings. They act out of ambition and greed. Their successes and failures, carefully analyzed, contained, it was believed, valuable lessons for political behavior. This was the kind of realism which could be found in the memoirs of Commines—and Commines, for La Popelinière's generation, came close to being an ideal type of historian.[26]

[23] Pierre Pithou, *Le premier livre des mémoires des comtes hereditaires de Champagne et Brie* (Paris, 1572), p. 1.

[24] La Popelinière, *Idée*, p. 22. When La Popelinière strung together these clichés from Cicero in 1599, he meant to ridicule the great herd of modern pedants who kept repeating these phrases sheepishly. But in his student days these affirmations of the importance of history were to be found in all the books and on the lips of all the masters.

[25] See Kelley, "Historia Integra," p. 35.

[26] For La Popelinière's judgment of Commines, together with the quoted opinions of Lipsius, see his *Histoire des histoires* (Paris, 1599), pp. 435–436.

However, shrewd political observations regarding the actions
of contemporary princes were one thing; to apply this kind of
political analysis to the past, to those dark centuries during
which only monks had recorded events, was another matter.
Here too the Italians had made some progress.

The *Decades* of Flavio Biondo, in particular, might serve as
a model for the reconstruction of that epoch, "from Orosius
onwards," when "events are obscure." Precisely because the
narrative sources for this period were rare and crude, Biondo
had been less tempted to stage-manage the affairs of Italy in
pseudoclassical style. He was even prodded, occasionally, into
using documents and archaeological materials. Not that he
practiced erudition out of principle; when his sources allowed
it, he composed set battle pieces and speeches with the best of
them. But when he wrote medieval history, because he was
"in the last resort, the victim rather than the master of his
sources," he abandoned the classical conventions: speeches
and extended battle descriptions became very rare, he was not
concerned with style, and he gave plenty of dates. There was
something to be learned from Biondo: his interest in the "dark
ages" in the first place, and then his respectful attitude toward
his sources. He was not uncritical; he was aware, for instance,
of the superior value of contemporary sources (*Nota auctor
proximus fuit his temporibus*). But when Biondo, "the first
medieval historian," decided to narrate a thousand years of
forgotten history, he was engaging in an activity neither fashionable nor rewarding in Italy.[27]

While ancient Rome and modern Florence could be used for
polemical purposes, the Italians had no use for their medieval past. Thus Biondo remained an antiquarian. "He was no
publicist. He had no argument to press; it is this which really
distinguishes him from a good many of his humanist contem-

On Fauchet's reading of Commines, see Espiner-Scott, *Fauchet*, p. 283; on
Masson's opinion of Commines, see Ronzy, *Masson*, p. 248.

[27] In all this I am following Denys Hay's fine essay, "Flavio Biondo and the
Middle Ages," *Proceedings of the British Academy* 45 (1959), pp. 97–125.

poraries. . . ." As Denys Hay has observed, Biondo's "sense of the conjunction of events" is not impressive. He has no point of view, no organizing principles for the history of medieval Italy. He follows one narrative source after another: Paulus Diaconus for the fifth century, Procopius for the Goths, and Ptolemy of Lucca from the ninth century on. He remains a compiler.[28] Hay suspects that Biondo was a shrewd enough commentator on politics and asks why he exercised his talents so rarely. Biondo was a servant of the pope, and this, argues Hay, accounts for his detachment. No doubt this could be, at least in part, the explanation. But even outside of the Curia there were no Italian historians to be found who cared enough about the Middle Ages to look at the sources with some question in mind. Valla's attack on the Donation of Constantine is the only exception which occurs to me. Neither Biondo nor Valla would have direct successors in Italy, but outside of Italy, the interests of nationalism and Protestantism would soon turn Biondo's antiquarian approach to the Middle Ages into history with a purpose.

Whatever the limitations of Italian Renaissance historical writing may have been, its achievements were very real and the Frenchmen were not blind to them. From the Italian humanists they learned methods of textual criticism; they learned that history was chiefly past politics, and only incidentally miracles and anecdotes; they learned to adopt a distant and ruthless attitude toward the medieval chroniclers; and they learned, if they needed to, the political uses of history.

All that they had learned from Italian literature was to be

[28] For the sources of the medieval books of the *Decades,* see Paul Buchholz, *Die Quellen der Historiarum Decades des Flavius Biondus* (Naumburg, 1881). A sample of Biondo's method is given in this description by Buchholz: "Biondus hat die Sammlung der 7 sog. Scriptores Hist. Aug. vor sich, geht die einzelnen Biographien durch, schreibt die Stellen an denen er einen Krieg mit den Goten—wenigstens nach seiner Vermuthung—erwähnt findet, meist wörtlich heraus—wo die Quelle lückenhaft ist, nimmt er Jordanis und Orosius zu Hand—und reiht so diese einzelnen Berichte meist locker, einförmig, wenig oder falsch motiviert aneinander." Buchholz, *Quellen der Historiarum Decades,* p. 9.

qualified during the next stage of their education, their apprenticeship at the schools of civil law where philology and jurisprudence were allied. There, under the aegis of Jacques Cujas, Andrea Alciato, Hotman, Baudouin, and other star professors, the new generation of French scholars was to receive its final and perhaps most important training. Their secondary education had prepared them for the formidable scholastic régime of the universities of Bourges, Valence, Orléans, and Toulouse. There the continued study of the classics of Greek and Latin literature was combined with the study of law. The masters of the law faculties were applying philological erudition and historical interpretation, in the manner of Budé, to the study of Roman law. Under this tutelage their students assimilated the methods, the interests, and the guiding principles of humanist jurisprudence.[29]

The jurists' approach to the detection of facts left an indelible mark on the method of the future historians.[30] It taught them the prime necessity of using original and authentic sources. Already introduced to the elements of textual criticism in the course of their humanist education in the colleges, they now learned to extend the principles of criticism to nonliterary sources. In comparison with the jurists' rigorous criteria of proof, the semifictional efforts of Emilio began to appear very unsatisfactory as historical work: "Let us grant Emilio the distinction of having been the most eloquent historian since Livy," writes Claude Fauchet, "but he was not the most trustworthy historian of France." Nicolas Vignier observed acidly

---

[29] On the French school of humanist jurisprudence and its influence on historical scholarship, see Kelley, "Historia Integra," "Fides Historiae," and "Budé"; Pocock, *Ancient Constitution and Feudal Law*; Bezold, *Aus Mittelalter und Renaissance*; Franklin, *Jean Bodin*; M. P. Gilmore, *Humanists and Jurists* (Cambridge, Mass., 1963); and Guido Kisch, *Humanismus und Jurisprudenz* (Basel, 1955).

[30] See, in this connection, J. Plattard's remarks on "l'empreinte de la profession juridique sur Montaigne": "veut-il se représenter la méthode idéale de l'historien dans la recherche de la vérité, il la conçoit comme une information judiciare." *La renaissance des lettres en France* (Paris, 1938), p. 55.

that most of the works on French history—especially those of
Emilio and his followers—were marred by the authors' ignorance of or contempt for chronology which resulted in their
losing sight of their subject "to the point of ending up high in
the air, above the clouds"; and from that insecure vantage
point "they give out with their lightweight, frivolous pointless
talk."[31] Something better was wanted: a "New History," no less,
the *"nouvelle histoire"* whose outline La Popelinière was to
commit to print in 1599.

The conviction that the old histories would not do and that
a breakthrough was needed was firmly implanted in the minds
of the leading scholars from the 1560s onwards. Was a new
history possible, a history which would not suffer from the
inanities ("niaiseries") of the old chroniclers and the frivoli-
ties of the Emilians? What kind of history would this be? Was
this "grave undertaking" beyond the means of human intelligence? To write the complete history of France (*historier
l'entier estat des affaires de France*),[32] to reduce, succinctly,
"into a single body" all the "principal substance of French history," "its causes and motives," according to chronological
order and according to the "histories, annals and chronicles
ancient and modern, printed and manuscript, foreign and
French, and according to the authentic charters and other
writings made under titles other than histories"[33]—this was
quite an undertaking.

The means for it were at hand, however, affirmed La Popelinière: "Graces à Dieu, les moyens sont à nostre porte." Looking around, he could see a "rare troupe" of great minds, among

---

[31] Fauchet's judgment is quoted in Espiner-Scott, *Fauchet*, p. 284. Vignier
writes: "Tellement qu'il se remarque en beaucoup d'endroits de nos histoires,
tant anciennes que modernes, notamment en celle de Paul Emile et de ceux
qui l'ont ensuivi, que l'ignorance ou mepris de l'ordre et des temps les a fait
égarer & voltiger par dessus les nuées . . . et de là discourir en l'air et à
l'adventure." Nicolas Vignier, *Sommaire de l'histoire des françois* (Paris,
1579), "Foreword to the Reader."

[32] La Popelinière, *La vraye et entiere histoire,* Preface.

[33] Vignier, *Sommaire,* Preface.

them several who were preparing themselves to become true historians (*se façonnans au modelle d'un vray historiographe*), historians of a new model such as had not been seen before. The New History, above all things, would *explain* events and explain them *completely*. Even the best of the older historians were "chroniqueurs" rather than "historiographes" because, as in the case of Johannes Sleidan, for example, their accounts were "too superficial and not instructive enough."[34] The New History would be "different from all histories seen so far"[35] precisely because it would explain all, and do it with a method so convincing that there could be no disagreement about the facts. The method, as Vignier explained, was to use all possible evidence, not merely narrative and literary sources, and to subject it to systematic criticism: "at every point one cites one's sources and determines when and where they originated," and "one lines them up chronologically to see how close they are to the events in question."[36] This was a difficult task, of course, and it could not be done without a certain amount of specialization and scholarly cooperation. Thus Vignier tells his readers that he has gone especially far in the elucidation and criticism of the sources from the ninth to the eleventh century in French history. He explains that his quotations of these sources and his critical comments are included in his book not only for the sake of truth but also to incite other scholars "to take better aim where I missed the target."[37]

After La Popelinière's demands for completeness in "perfect history," Vignier, writing in 1579, must preface his work with

[34] La Popelinière, *La vraye et entiere histoire*, Preface.

[35] *Loc. cit.*

[36] "Ie nomme pareillement à chacun bout de chãp mes aucteurs & garants avec le lieu & l'année ou chacun de ceux qui ont escrit de nostre France a commencé & finy son oeuvre, les faisant venir en rang les uns apres les autres, selon qu'ils ont plus approché des temps pour la preuve desquels ie les employe. . . ." Vignier, *Sommaire*, Preface.

[37] ". . . tant pour favoriser la verité, que pour inciter les esprits studieux de l'antiquité de viser mieux où ils cognoistront que ie n'auray bien atteint." *Loc. cit.*

a modest disclaimer: "this little piece of work" (*ce mien petit labeur*) is not, as yet, an "histoire entière de la France"; but, such as it is, it is entirely new, there has never been anything like it before.[38]

Vignier and La Popelinière were claiming the discovery of a method which was to make sense of the history of France, to explain its course in its entirety, and to support these explanations with solid and irrefutable documentary proof. The fancies of the chroniclers and the fantasies of the men of letters were to be superseded by the rigorous detective work of the philologists and jurists. To see how much truth there is to these claims, let us turn to the researches of one of the most successful exponents of the new kind of history, Estienne Pasquier.

---

[38] ". . . un simple recueil en forme d'Annales, tel toutes fois (i'ose dire) qu'aucun autre ne nous a encores fait voir." *Loc. cit.*

The researches
of
Estienne Pasquier

Third chapter

Forty years ago, when R. G. Collingwood addressed himself to the question of the origins of modern historical science,
he wrote that "In the sense in which Gibbon and Mommsen
were historians, there was no such thing as an historian before
the 18th century." He meant that history before the eighteenth

This chapter was originally published in a somewhat different
French version under the title "Naissance de l'histoire en France:
Les "Recherches" d'Estienne Pasquier" in *Annales: Economies,
sociétés, civilisations* 23 (1968), pp. 69–105.

century had been, on the whole, nothing but the records of contemporary observations piled one on top of the other by more or less reliable annalists. This sort of activity, in Collingwood's view, had little in common with the work of the modern historian whose discipline he defined as "a study at once critical and constructive, whose field is the human past in its entirety, and whose method is the reconstruction of the past from documents written and unwritten, critically analyzed and interpreted." This very sharp distinction between modern and pre-modern historiography has been, it seems to me, a useful exaggeration. With this assumption as a starting point, students of historiography have tried to explain why the modern conception of history did not come into existence earlier. But I think it is time to shift to a new approach and to ask just exactly how this revolution came about. Modern history may well have been "an absolutely new movement in the life of mankind,"[1] but it cannot have come into being suddenly, in the course of a generation. So complex an upheaval in the history of thought must have been the slow product of its own history.

To say that any history, in the modern sense of the word, was being written before the eighteenth century, is to state a controversial thesis. Of course there were historians then, but they were writers of contemporary or near-contemporary history, statesmen usually, who recorded and analyzed the world they moved in (Commines, Guicciardini, De Thou). Their fame in their own time and since has rested on their literary ability, on their access to information, and on the intelligence of their observations. Their works are sources for the history of their own time, and they were intended as such.

To write contemporary history is one thing: any fool can do it, as A. D. Momigliano observed some time ago.[2] Such a writer, if he is not a fool, does something difficult and useful, but his

[1] R. G. Collingwood, *Speculum Mentis* (Oxford, 1924), p. 204. Also see his *The Idea of History* (Oxford, 1946), p. 209.

[2] A. D. Momigliano, *Histoire et historiens dans l'antiquité* (Geneva, 1958), p. 27.

activity has very little in common with that of the historian who asks questions about the past, any portion of the past, and attempts to answer these questions through the interpretation of documents, written or unwritten. Were there such historians?

Until about 1560 the answer is that there were probably no such historians. This is not to say that the educated person of this time had no interest in the past. On the contrary, the past was a matter of passionate concern to him, as it had been to European intellectuals since at least the third century of our era.[3] Since the fourteenth century the hitherto blurred distinction between past and present had come into sharp focus. In Italy, especially, the documents of pagan and Christian antiquity had been recovered and the ancient past, as a result, was perceived more clearly, if not more critically. At the beginning of the sixteenth century, European intellectuals knew the history of the ancient Hebrews, Greeks, and Romans at first hand, that is, from the testimony of the ancient historians, whose works were available as they had never been before, in excellent editions, even in translation, and provided with learned commentaries.

Yet, with all that, there were no historians of antiquity. The ancient literary texts provided a consistent picture of the events that mattered. With those in hand, every educated man became his own historian. At most he required the help of the philologists to clarify some obscure passage, or the help of the antiquarian who could occasionally fill out the gaps between the narrative histories with the help of legal documents, monuments, coins, and inscriptions. Ancient history had been written once and for all by the Ancients. Not before the end of the century would this proposition be questioned.

In the meantime, there were certainly other epochs, less fortunate in this respect than antiquity, whose history had not been written. The Turks or the Americans, lacking a literary

[3] See the interesting remarks of Philippe Ariès in *Le temps de l'histoire* (Monaco, 1954), pp. 100–102, on the birth of historical-mindedness in Roman culture.

tradition of their own, certainly presented an inviting target for a modern Herodotus. But what about the more immediate, the more practical field of European medieval history? Did it, or did it not, require historians?

The solid picture presented by ancient history helped to underline the chaotic condition of medieval history. Not only the historical literature but the very events of the Middle Ages seemed to lack the cohesion which distinguished ancient history. Since the fifth century history was no longer the history of a people, of a city, or even of an empire. Only by seeking the transcendental meaning of this history could one make sense of it, but to the man for whom history was Thucydides and Tacitus, the lives of saints seemed irrelevant. If history was the study of the state, then the monks spoke of it "as blind men speak of color."[4]

What was to be done? Should one simply shrug off a thousand years of one's past as incomprehensible, once and for all, because of the failure of generations of annalists? Some could do this, either because the lives of saints outweighed the lives of generals, in their estimation, as a fit subject for history, or because, in their view, no history mattered since the fall of Rome. But these two schools of otherworldliness were challenged. New perspectives on church history, colored by Protestantism, and new perspectives on political history, colored by nationalism, sought to reshape the history of the Middle Ages.

In France the need to reinterpret medieval history manifested itself very sharply after the death of King Henri II in 1559 and during the troubled years that followed, when French society underwent a profound constitutional crisis. Suddenly threatened, the most venerable institutions in the kingdom had to be justified. The sanction of the church, the sanction of the crown, the sanction of the university no longer sufficed: even these pillars of society were in danger of crumbling. Authority lay in antiquity. The monarchy, then, the church, and all other

[4] As Pithou put it in *Mémoires*, p. 1.

institutions would have to be traced back to their origins, justified through history. For this purpose the old chronicles were useless. A new history was needed, a history at once consistent and founded in fact, and a history which could provide certainties safe from the attacks of skeptics and political propagandists: in short, a history of France which would be the equal of the history of Rome.

The publication of the *Recherches*

The new history which tried to meet these standards can be dated from the publication of the first book of Estienne Pasquier's *Recherches de la France* (1560). In this self-consciously new history Pasquier took the view that there were no medieval historians. The narrative records of that age were to be treated as raw materials for the writing of history. They were what we would call primary sources, no better—often worse—than other sources such as legal documents or folk tradition. There were no authorities to follow in this field, no secondary sources as we would call them.

The most practical and immediate implication of this point of view was that there was no accepted story outline. A generation earlier the outline of the old royal chronicles had sufficed even for a sophisticated Italian like Paolo Emilio, whose version of French history remained mostly a classical version of the *Grandes Chroniques*. Emilio and all the chroniclers and historians who preceded him since the seventh century began the history of France with the legendary descent of the Franks from the Trojan heroes. Emilio did not even believe this tale, but he knew of no other way of beginning an account of the history of France.[5]

To those who picked up Pasquier's book in 1560, the novelty of the work must have been immediately obvious. It is likely

[5] Emilio, *De rebus gestis Francorum,* Liber I, Fo. III. On Emilio's history and its relation to the *Grandes Chroniques* see Davies, "Late XVth Century French Historiography."

that Pasquier's public was largely limited to likeminded readers: his colleagues in the courts of law, gentlemen or bourgeois, royal officers, many of them endowed with solid classical educations and most of them trained in civil law at the same universities. Pasquier's interest in French antiquities, his speculations about the nature of French laws and customs, these were the common talk of the earnest *salons* where these lawyers came together. Even these men, to whom the substance of Pasquier's researches was familiar, found his method radical.

Some thirty years later, in a preface to another edition of his *Recherches*, Pasquier recalled the atmosphere of the 1560s when his first book came out. Before publication he had, naturally, circulated the manuscript among his friends, asking for their criticism and advice. According to Pasquier, the most constant criticism he received was directed at his habit of referring very frequently to the sources he was quoting. This device, his critics thought, reminded one too much of the "darkness of the schools" and hardly seemed fitting in a work of history. Was it really necessary, they asked, to refer to these sources? If it was a question of giving authority and credence to his account, this would come in good time. Literature, like gold, acquired a fine patina with age. After all, the works of the Ancients were not encumbered with quotations and yet, in time, they had acquired authority. Why should this not happen to Pasquier's work in the future?[6]

---

[6] "Communiquant ces presentes Recherches à mes amis . . . il y en avoit quelques uns qui trouvoient de mauvaise grace qu'à chaque bout de champ ie confirmasse mon dire par quelque autheur ancien . . ."; ". . . le temps affinoit comme l'or, les oeuvres . . ."; "toutes fois à l'advenir elles pourroient s'authoriser d'elles mesmes, ainsi qu'il en estoit advenu aux anciens. . . ." Estienne Pasquier, *Recherches de la France*, p. 1. All references, unless otherwise noted, are to the edition of 1607 published in Paris by Laurent Sonnius. This is the last edition whose printing was supervised by Pasquier (it was reprinted in 1611 and 1617). The posthumous editions contain additional essays, including an entire book on the history of universities. For a detailed bibliography of Pasquier's works, see D. Thickett, *Bibliographie des oeuvres d'Etienne Pasquier* (Geneva, 1956) in *Travaux d'humanisme et Renaissance,* no. 21.

In 1560 these were neither frivolous nor cynical comments.
They simply reflected the current understanding in humanist
circles of what history-writing was about. It was, first of all,
literature; factual accuracy was not a prime concern; and it
was written for posterity. Now, Pasquier's purposes were quite
different. He was not indifferent to style, but he thought of his
activity as, first and foremost, a reconstruction of the past for
the needs of the present, and a reconstruction which would be
worthless if it did not aim at achieving a degree of certainty
beyond dispute.

Some of Pasquier's friends accepted the principle of referring
to sources but advised against quoting lengthy extracts from
the documents. Their argument, that this practice came close
to plagiarism, did not convince Pasquier. To be sure, many of
the documents he was quoting had been seen by his predecessors, but "seen without being seen"; that is to say, they may have
seen them without understanding their significance. For this
reason, Pasquier did not think it at all superfluous to quote his
sources at length. Since his interpretations had nothing in common with those of the traditional annalists, people might think
he was making up a new history of France. Therefore he
adopted a method which consisted in "saying nothing of importance without proving it" and in showing his readers the
"sources which were at the root of his conjectures." He found
it necessary not only to show what France had been like in
ancient times, but almost to have his readers "touch it with their
fingers."[7]

Pasquier liked the role of innovator. He described the novelty
of his historical method in a simile taken from the world of the

---

[7] ". . . tous ces passages avoiët esté veuz par noz predecesseurs sans les
voir . . ."; "Et parce qu'és discours de toutes ces particularitez j'apportois
opinions non aucunement touchees ou recogneues par ceux qui avoiët escrit
noz Annales, ie pensay les authoriser par les anciens, dont i'avois recueilly
mes coniectures"; ". . . ie me suis resolu de ne rien dire qui importe, sans en
faire preuve . . ."; "ce n'estoit assez de monstrer quelle fust l'ancienneté de
nostre France, ains la faire toucher au doigt, alleguant tantost les autheurs,
tantost couchant leurs passages tout au long." Pasquier, *Recherches*, pp. 2, 3.

Arctic explorers: his method was so successful, he tells us, that an entire squadron of French intellectuals began to follow in his wake—which was easy enough, he adds, the first ice being broken.[8] I am not sure one can accuse him of exaggeration here. To be sure, he did not invent historical criticism. The method he advocated had been practiced before him by, among others, Valla, Poliziano, Erasmus, Budé, Alciato, Cujas, Beatus Rhenanus, Baudouin, and Hotman. Indeed, Pasquier and his generation had learned it from these masters, but in Pasquier's book the historical method of the jurists and the philologists was applied for the first time to the problems of French history. The consequences proved fateful.

There had never been a book about French history that even remotely resembled the small volume published in 1560. Even the title was new: not a history of France, but "researches" in French history. What did the author mean by "researches"? A quick leafing through the volume would show that the method was that of the learned essays of the philologists. The author, however, wrote in French, not Latin. Even the quotations from Latin texts were translated into French. The style was easy, colloquial, and imaginative. Clearly, here was a scholar who was taking the trouble to reach a large public.

The general subject of this first book of *Recherches* (the author promised more to follow later) was the earliest history of France. One would naturally expect to find, on the very first page, the hallowed names of Priam, Hector, and Francio, the Trojan ancestors of the Franks. No history of French origins had appeared yet without such a beginning. If the reader already knew of Pasquier and of his circle, he might be prepared for a witty demonstration of the absurdity of the Trojan legend. In the *Recherches*, however, the reader found neither Trojans nor Franks, for Pasquier began with the Gauls.[9]

[8] *Ibid.,* p. 2.

[9] To appreciate just how much of a revolutionary step this was, one need only read the French medievalist Ferdinand Lot, who, in his estimation of early modern historiography, makes the perfectly common mistake of assuming

Pasquier asks himself the question: where does the history of France begin? So far, all those who had asked this question seemed to have answered it in the same way; the history of France begins, of course, where the chroniclers begin it. They might have gone on from there and found the chroniclers' account of French origins too implausible; they might have argued with it, even rejected it and skipped a few pages, and started their story at a point in the older text which seemed more believable—skipped Francio, for instance, and moved on to Pharamond.

Pasquier managed to get away from earlier historiographical conventions completely. There is not a word about the Gauls in the chronicles. Where then did he find them? He found them in Julius Caesar. To look for the origins of French history in Caesar's account of his wars in Gaul may seem to us a fairly natural decision. To make this decision, however, Pasquier had to abandon one concept of historiography and create a new one. Instead of thinking of the writing of history as an editorial task, he thought of it as a scientific task. Instead of rewriting a traditional body of chronicles, he began with a question and sought its answer.

The needs of French nationalism

Before he took this step, the history of France had been a special subject, a legendary theme which could be used for literary or iconographic purposes, of which new versions could be made but whose fundamental stories and characters remained unchanged. As Philippe Ariès puts it, the History of France was a "privileged period which began with the first king,

---

that the Gauls were unknown to historians before the eighteenth century: "When does the history of France begin? That is a question our ancestors did not ask. For them the history of our country began with the arrival of the Franks. . . ." "They did not even ask themselves who inhabited Gaul before that time, or rather they answered: the Romans. . . ." *La Gaule* (Paris, 1947), p. 7.

Pharamond, already a king exactly like all the other kings to come, and this privileged period was set outside of time. . . . Nothing comes before; there was once a king of France."[10]

This romantic and heroic version of the past must have exerted a strong and lasting appeal, since its popularity continued through the nineteenth century. The heroes of this epic were kings and saints, bishops and knights. Its stock situations were battles and miracles, its most scientific aspects, heraldry and genealogy. It appealed, of course, to kings, bishops, and knights. And it also appealed to saints; it was this folkloric version of French history that animated Joan of Arc's patriotism.

Pasquier and his colleagues were able to resist the charm of these stories because they were outsiders. Powerful and wealthy as they were, these magistrates were neither warriors nor priests; they would have looked in vain for mention of their ancestors in the *Grandes Chroniques.* Nor were they interested in battles and miracles. The things they were interested in, alas, had not interested the chroniclers. Those old "rappetasseurs," those incompetent compilers, could only produce a history without substance, "fantosmes d'histoire."[11]

Just as the medieval commentators had obscured the meaning of Roman law, so the chroniclers had obscured the meaning of French history. The remedy, which was working so well in the field of law, could work in the field of history too: the return to the original sources, *ad fontes.* Pasquier as a bourgeois, as a lawyer, as a humanist could reason thus; but it was Pasquier the nationalist who went straight to the Gauls and identified them as his ancestors, founding thereby a nationalism independent of the royal dynasties. Pasquier's decision to begin the history of France with the Gauls clearly implied that France existed before and separately from its kings, its church, its

[10] Ariès, *Le temps de l'histoire,* p. 195.

[11] Pasquier, *Lettres,* p. 275. All references to the *Lettres,* unless otherwise noted, are to the last edition of the *Oeuvres* (Amsterdam, 1723) of which they form vol. II.

Frankish nobility, and Rome. What was France? A people distinct from others through its institutions.

Pasquier begins his essay on the Gauls by lamenting the absence of historical records. The Gauls were derelict in this respect. To reconstruct their history is therefore a very difficult task. All one could do was to sift through the reports of outsiders, most of them worthless and all of them hostile. Still, enough was left so that one could get a glimpse of their customs and institutions.

Were the Gauls barbarians, as the Italians would have it? Caesar, the only Roman writer whose testimony is firsthand, is more respectful of the Gauls than all the other writers. In fact, Caesar only calls us barbarians twice in the course of his book, Pasquier notes. But even on those two occasions we are dealing with impulsive opinions. To find out just how civilized the Gauls were, one must study the entire text of Caesar's book, although Caesar shows the Gauls from an odd, biased perspective and often tells us things without wanting to. Pasquier clearly treats Caesar as a primary source. Typically, after a long quotation, he stops to address the reader: "Indeed here is what Caesar says in passing. But what shall we extract out of it?"[12]

What he does extract out of Caesar is a sketch of the customs and institutions of the Gauls which is consistent with the evidence, but also consistently favorable. Caesar accuses the Gauls of being frivolous, volatile, unreliable. But, Pasquier suggests, because they seemed unreliable to a Roman general, we must not necessarily conclude that there was something wrong with their character. Their constant intrigues and revolts can be explained by the political circumstances, that is, their desire for freedom from Roman oppression. As for the degree of civilization existing in Gaul, Pasquier concludes that it was higher than that existing among the Britons and the Germans; as Caesar saw them, the Gauls were the least barbarous of the western

---

[12] ". . . bien qu'à la traverse & peut estre, sans y penser il nous en ait doñé les Memoires"; "En effect voila que Cesar dit en passant. Mais que tirons nous de cecy." Pasquier, *Recherches*, p. 14.

barbarians. There were good reasons, Pasquier thinks, for the Gauls' superiority: they had better institutions. In fact, their institutions were so good that they survived the Roman and Germanic conquests and still existed, in one form or another.

If we stop here to take stock, we can see that Pasquier set out to reconstruct a portion of the distant past which had never had a history. No historians had recorded the earliest centuries of French history. Only the fantasies of late writers were extant. These could be dismissed, and one was obliged to start from scratch. The materials available for such a task were certainly inadequate. No one had bothered "to reconstruct for us a king in all his functions, analyzing the deliberations and councils and narrating for us in carefully chosen words the decisions and actions and their results so that we can picture it all as if we had been there in person."[13] In other words, no one had done for the French what Thucydides had done for the Athenians. To rectify this injustice is Pasquier's avowed aim.

He admits, however, that this is not always possible, especially for the earliest period in French history. The most he can hope to accomplish is to imagine what the Gauls were like from a study of their customs as reported by Caesar, just as the "hunter imagines the size of the deer from his tracks."[14] A rough sketch of the institutions and customs of his ancestors is all he can hope to reconstruct. Even so, the information available is so scarce and uncertain that no one can speak of these things except "by conjectures which grow out of our own particular judgment," and are "controlled by our individual passions."[15]

What then does Pasquier expect to gain from his researches? Even the first page of his book gives us the answer: he expects to prove the historical continuity of certain fundamental in-

[13] *Ibid.*, p. 7.

[14] *Ibid.*, p. 6

[15] *Ibid.*, p. 196.

stitutions. One might go even further and say that his researches
are an attempt to define the French constitution through its
history. Pasquier is not an antiquarian: one must flee the antiquarian impulse in his opinion, "as one flees shoals at sea."[16]
He is not a collector of historical information: he uses history.

The *mos Gallicus*

Pasquier learned to use history in the law schools. It was in
1546 in Paris that he first heard the lectures of two of the ablest
young exponents of the *mos Gallicus*, the reforming movement
in legal studies which had swept the civil law faculties of France.
Those lectures, by Baudouin and Hotman, made a profound
impression on the seventeen-year-old Pasquier. He went on to
Toulouse and heard the lectures of Cujas, who was to become
the master of this movement. Then he went to Italy to hear
Alciato at Pavia.[17] From these jurists, Pasquier acquired both a
practical method for the interpretation of documents and a philosophy of history.

The method was that of the philologists who, since the publication of Guillaume Budé's *De asse* (1515), had been renew-
ing classical studies and transforming the study of Roman
law.[18] Budé's work pointed the way for a new understanding of
Roman history which had appeared until then mostly as a collection of edifying biographies. In his concern with the every-
day material reality of Roman life, Budé was able to see beyond
the majestic façade erected in the pages of the Roman historians. His insight into the Roman economy led him to observe
that "all the evidence collected in this book makes Rome ap-

[16] "Non pas pour nous rendre antiquaires (. . . ie suis d'avis qu'il faut fuir
cela comme un banc ou ecueil en pleine mer)." Pasquier, *Lettres* (1619), I,
p. 107.

[17] *Ibid.*, p. 568.

[18] On Budé, see Delaruelle, *Guillaume Budé*, and Kelley, "Budé."

pear as the home base of robbers who have succeeded in laying waste the whole world. . . ."[19]

Budé demonstrated that the critique of texts combined with archaeological techniques could lead to an accurate representation of the past. Following his lead, philologists and jurists, especially those associated with the law faculties of Orléans, Valence, and Bourges, edited texts and studied coins, charters, inscriptions, and chronology. The focus of these studies remained Rome and its laws. In theory, however, there was no reason to limit the application of the historical method to Roman law. Through the study of history, Budé and his disciples claimed, the secrets of the laws of all peoples at all times could be understood.[20] As early as 1519, Juan Luis Vives expressed this conviction in the phrase: "Jus totum manat ex historia."[21] But it was only in the 1560s that younger men like Baudouin and Bodin seriously explored the application of the historical method outside of the field of Roman law.[22] Eventually, the historical method which had been developed for the purpose of understanding Roman law became a tool for the understanding of all laws. History became a social science in the law schools.

Nationalism and historicism

That was Pasquier's understanding: the rise and fall of states could be explained and even predicted by a specialist with methods as "tangible [*palpables*] as mathematical demonstrations."[23] Such statements of absolute confidence in the scientific

---

[19] Guillaume Budé, *De asse*, p. 169, quoted by Delaruelle, *Guillaume Budé*, p. 146.

[20] J. Bohatec, *Budé und Calvin* (Graz, 1950), p. 17.

[21] Quoted by Bezold, "Zur Entstehungsgeschichte der historischen Methodik," p. 370.

[22] See Kelley, "Historia Integra," p. 35; see also Franklin, *Bodin*.

[23] Pasquier, *Recherches*, p. 37.

possibilities of historical research are rare in his work, however.
The jurists taught him to interpret documents. They also taught
him that from such interpretations one could reconstruct the
historical setting which had produced these documents. There
was, then, a satisfactory method for historical explanation and
there was no need to look for outside factors. While divine
providence surely played an important part in determining
human affairs, it was a mysterious agent, and there was no need
to invoke it as long as the events and their causes could be reconstructed from the sources.

Pasquier pays only lip service to divine providence and Fortuna as factors in historical causation. A typical case is his
essay on "Which of the two, Fortuna or Policy, has been more
important in the perpetuation of this kingdom of France." He
begins this essay by allowing that it seems miraculous that
France alone, of all the states established by the Germanic
conquests, should have lasted so long. He lists several of the
more important instances when the kingdom seemed on the
verge of ruin, from the death of Clovis to the Hundred Years'
War, and concludes that France has been saved again and again
by Fortune. "When I speak of Fortune," he adds prudently, "let
it be understood, so that no one has occasion to be scandalized,
that I mean the mysteries of God which cannot be discovered
by our human prudence." Having made this concession to his
more orthodox readers, perhaps to lull the suspicions aroused
by the Machiavellian title of his essay, he then quietly proceeds
to argue his thesis, which is, of course, that policy is responsible
for France's good fortune.[24] Less respectable determinisms,
among others the popular theory that climate influences civilization, Pasquier exposes as fallacious. "Get rid of this mad
notion," he writes in 1554 to a friend, "that climate makes
people more or less cultured, as if there were some countries
where good letters flourish more naturally." That this notion
is false

[24] *Ibid.*, pp. 69–73.

can be seen from very clear "ocular examples." Was there ever country more favored with great men in science and in other fields than Greece? Was there ever such barbarity in the world as is true now? Or take Africa: was it ever considered civilized by the Ancients? Yet, shortly after the coming of Christianity, was there ever a country in the world that produced greater doctors of the Church than Africa? Or again, was there ever a country as uncivilized as Germany, at the time of the Roman republic? In this same country today, and for the past century or so, all disciplines flourish with excellence. Clearly then, it is practice and vigilance that produce culture, not the natural conditions of a region.

Just why civilizations rise and fall Pasquier could not be sure, but he has made one observation, namely, that when "kingdoms or states are first established, you will find that arms, not letters, flourish. . . ." But when these states "begin to grow and reach their maturity, it happens frequently that culture begins to be appreciated and then, with the decline of the state, culture also declines. It is true that this last point is not all that certain . . . ," he concludes, since there have been great states devoid of culture.[25]

Pasquier was not tempted by grandiose schemes of historical explanation. Perhaps it was his mania for facts which kept him away from the level of abstraction on which men like Bodin pursued their discourses. Already as a young man in his twenties, before the composition of the first *Recherches*, Pasquier was gathering facts with, it would seem, no precise aim in mind. For example, according to a letter he wrote later in life, he was riding back to Paris from his country house one day in 1556 when he met a friend in Melun who persuaded him to interrupt his journey in order to visit an acquaintance. When they arrived at this man's house, they met a Jesuit who was staying there. Pasquier, neglecting his social duties and forgetting the purpose of his trip, had only one thought in mind: he knew nothing about the Society of Jesus, and here was a first-rate informant available to him. He accosted the Jesuit and asked him to tell

[25] Pasquier, *Lettres*, pp. 9–10.

him all he knew of the origins and progress of the Company.
The Jesuit obliged and the two locked themselves into a room
for two consecutive days. Pen, ink, and paper in hand, Pasquier filled three or four great sheets, taking down what the
Jesuit was willing to tell him. Afterwards, he put the notes
somewhere among his files.[26]

However, Pasquier was not collecting data as aimlessly as it
would appear. From the start he made the decision to concern
himself with the history of France alone. Rome, its history and
its laws, he affects to despise as a subject for historical research.
The history of France, he contends, is a subject in no way in-
ferior to the history of Rome.[27] As for Roman law, the French
would be better off without it.[28] The architectural remains of
Rome, cherished by generations of European intellectuals, seem
to him worthless.[29] The use of Latin quotations in modern
works of literature seems to him a bad habit; it smacks of
pedantry.[30] His taste in architecture is nationalist too; the most
beautiful buildings in Paris, in his opinion, are the Sainte
Chapelle, the Cathedral of Notre Dame, and the Palace of Jus-

---

[26] *Ibid.*, p. 683.

[27] *Ibid.*, p. 28.

[28] ". . . je ne sçay si nous ne ferions aussi bien de nous passer de ceste
curiosité des Loix Romaines, ayans les nostres au point. . . ." Pasquier, "Pourparler du Prince," *Recherches*, p. 1130.

[29] In a letter in which he recommends his son to Monsieur de Foix in Rome,
he expresses the opinion that "ces antiquailles de Rome" "ne me semblent de
grande edification . . ." for his son's education; he would prefer to have him
consider "les images vifves, dont il pourra rapporter un exemple & modelle
de bien vivre à l'advenir." Pasquier, *Lettres*, p. 172.

[30] Writing to his friend Loysel, he criticizes his style as tactfully as possible:
". . . je vous prie prendre de bonne part ce que je veux vous mander main-
tenant . . . : ce que vous estimez le plus riche en icelles [his speeches], est,
à mon jugement, le plus pauvre; je veux dire, tant de passages Grecs &
Latins, tant d'allegations d'autheurs, dont vous reparez vostre discours: je
desire que . . . nous habillions un Orateur à la Françoise, si proprement &
à propos, que nos actions s'eslongnent le plus qu'elles pourront, de la poul-
siere des escholes. . . ." *Ibid.*, pp. 191–192.

tice, buildings which, the architects assure him, have no trace of Greek or Roman style.[31]

Pasquier is an avowed propagandist for the history of France, its literature, its laws, and its institutions. Is his nationalism an obsession, is it mere chauvinism that makes him reject Rome, and how, if this were true, could his treatment of French history retain enough objectivity to make positive contributions to historical knowledge?

There is nothing more striking in the *Recherches* than the calm and conciliatory tone in which Pasquier handles controversial questions. Lively and colloquial by the dull standards of twentieth-century scholarly writing, the *Recherches* will impress anyone familiar with the strident tones of sixteenth-century scholarly controversy as a model of dignity. The typical French chauvinist of the period spoke in other tones, loudly proclaimed the glorious descent of his compatriots from the seed of Priam or some other illustrious hero, and vociferously damned France's enemies. Pasquier is courteous throughout and never loses his sense of humor. He does not glorify the history of France and he does not heap glamour upon its kings, as do all the paid panegyrists of the century. After his death he was vilified by a Jesuit precisely on the ground that he was not respectful enough of the honor of French kings. His *Recherches* in the eyes of seventeenth-century courtiers seemed a *corpus* of *lèse-majesté*.[32] The fact is that Pasquier the nationalist can consistently view the history of France more objectively than most of his contemporaries. His anti-Romanism does not proceed from simple xenophobia; his French researches are not to be confused with a glorification of France. Both proceed from the historicist teaching of the Cujas school.

---

[31] *Ibid.* Not that he despises Roman architecture; he finds the newly built Louvre beautiful too, embodying, as it does, the best of the classical style. What Pasquier insists on is the distinctiveness of French architecture which owes no debt to Rome, in his opinion.

[32] The Jesuit Garasse devoted a 985-page volume, *Les recherches des Recherches et autres oeuvres de Me. Estienne Pasquier* (Paris, 1622) to this thesis.

Pasquier had learned from the jurists that there is nothing
absolute about laws, that they are merely the customs of a society written down at some time.[33] Since society and its needs
change constantly, as do language and all other things, this
perpetual *mutation* (one of his favorite words) makes laws obsolete and requires that they be constantly reformed.[34] Laws
are different everywhere and often contradictory, even within
a single country, and their slow evolution is the product of
time.[35] That law is merely the product of history, that customs
change, these are the lessons he learned from the study of
Roman law. He drew the conclusion that Roman laws and
Roman values were obsolete. Rome was a dead society. Its
remains, embedded in French law, were fossil remains. It was
pointless to use the Latin language when the French would
do.[36] For the same reason, it was more useful to study the institutions of France than those of Rome, since France was alive
and Rome of interest only to antiquarians.

Pasquier turned away from classical history because he was
an activist by circumstances and by temperament. He lived
at a fateful moment in the history of the world and he understood this clearly. A colleague of his at the Bordeaux *parlement*
had summed up the sixteenth century thus: "All the world
was peaceful, there were no religious disputes, everyone lived
in peace in his corner, followed the faith of his ancestors, and

[33] Pasquier, *Lettres*, p. 577.

[34] The constant *mutation* of society and of its laws is one of the main
themes of the *Recherches*. Sample statements may be found in the *Recherches*, 1569 edition, on pp. 135, 156, 160, 224. On language change, also a
theme in the *Recherches*, see the letter to Cujas in which he discusses the
perils of translation and points out how language changes: "Cependant petit
à petit sa langue maternelle se change de telle façon avec le temps, que
comme si nous luy avions baillé une robbe neufve, nous ne voulons plus
user de la vieille." Pasquier, *Lettres*, p. 37.

[35] ". . . Les Coustumes se forment en chasque pays, petit à petit, de la diversité de nos moeurs & nos moeurs de la diversité de nos esprits. . . ."
Pasquier, *Lettres*, p. 225.

[36] A point he stresses frequently. See, among others, his letter to Turnèbe,
written in 1552, *Lettres*, pp. 3–8.

fought only for territorial gains. Suddenly, at the beginning of the sixteenth century, everything fell apart, Christendom was divided by sects and heresies which covered the earth with misery and desolation, in Asia and Africa and Europe." To this appreciation of the revolution of his time, Pasquier proposed that he should add the revolution in science brought about by "three great men (innovators or heretics, if you like) who came to upset tradition: Copernicus, Paracelsus and Ramus."[37]

Everything in Pasquier's upbringing, in his education, in his work at the *parlement* prompted him to see the disorders of his time as especially acute and destructive in the realm of French politics. The troubles, which began openly in 1559 and which continued throughout the century, had to be understood before they could be cured. It seemed the proper function of magistrates like himself, *gens de robe longue*, to perform this task of analysis. In the presence of several conflicting interpretations of the French constitution, Pasquier's reflex was to establish beyond reasonable doubt what the nature of this constitution was. Historical research was the solution. To understand what were the rights of the crown, of the church, of the *parlement*, of the Estates, of royal officers, one had to understand how these institutions had grown up in time. Avoiding all speculations as to what any given law or custom ought to be, Pasquier only asked how it came to be.

As was already clear in his treatment of the Gauls, in his choice of the Gauls as the first French people, Pasquier does not interrogate the sources without some preconceived notions. He is looking for the sources of the French constitution, but he already has a fairly clear idea of what he wishes to find. In the first place he hates absolutism in all its forms. The French monarchy, he is determined to prove, has always submitted to some form of constitutional limitation. The assemblies of the nobles in Celtic Gaul or in the Merovingian kingdom performed the necessary function of advising kings, as does the

[37] *Ibid.*, p. 605.

parlement in his time. While the monarch in the French constitution is not responsible to such an assembly, he is nevertheless guided by its remonstrances.[38] Pasquier gives the *parlement* a very large role in the history of France. In this instance
perhaps more than in any other, he lets his political and social
prejudices color his reconstruction of national history.

At the beginning of his researches he asks the fundamental
question: why did the French state alone, of all the barbarian
kingdoms which flourished in the ruins of the empire, survive
continuously to the present day? He answers by attributing
this success not to Fortuna, divine providence, or accident, but
to a series of wise decisions made by men. The first Frankish
kings wisely left Gallo-Roman institutions untouched, for the
most part. Clovis' conversion to Christianity was a move of
profound political wisdom: the conqueror thus attached the
Christian Gauls to his cause. The Merovingian mayors of the
palace, because they needed broad support for their coup
d'état against the legitimate kings, held annual meetings of the
nobility and thus already mixed aristocracy with monarchy.[39]
From political move to political move in the course of centuries,
despite relapses here and there, French society, as Pasquier
saw it, held together because of the heritage of a mixed constitution, because of the flexibility of its statesmen who succeeded,
in one form or another, in maintaining this important balance
and continuing the fundamental, almost natural, laws which

---

[38] On the mixed constitution of France and on the wisdom of the kings of
France who "reduisans parce moyen leur puissance absoluë sous la civilité
de la loy . . ." have thus ". . . conservé leur grandeur successivement depuis
onze cents ans iusques à huy." *Ibid.*, pp. 145–146. On his hatred of absolutism: "Vray Dieu, que ce Quadrain de Monsieur de Pibrac me plaist: Ie
hay ces mots de puissance absoluë / De plain pouvoir, de propre mouve-
ment /. . . ." *Ibid.*, p. 155.

[39] "Lequel des deux, de la Fortune ou du Conseil, a plus ouvré à la
manutention de ce Royaume de France" is the topic of the first chapter of
Book II of the *Recherches* (p. 69) and, in effect, the topic of the entire
Book. On Clovis' attitude toward Gallo-Roman institutions, including the
Christian church, see *ibid.*, p. 71; on Merovingian representative assemblies,
see *ibid.*, p. 72.

had always governed the life of the French nation. The answer to the question he poses at the beginning of his researches can be found in the entire book, as it grew over some sixty-five years. The success of France, so far, has depended on the strength of its institutions, and foremost among these, the *parlement* in its various forms.

Pasquier, however, is not a political theorist. One can derive a constitutional theory from the *Recherches* only by implication, only by piecing together casual observations, by observing his emphases. There are two essays on the history of the *parlement* in the earliest edition of Book II of the *Recherches*. The first is a short historical sketch of the *placita*, the assemblies of various sorts which fulfilled, Pasquier suggests, something like the function of the modern *parlement*. Using whatever sources he can get his hands on, always preferring the testimony of contemporaries, Pasquier sees in the irregularly held assemblies of the Merovingian, Carolingian, and Capetian kings the indispensable cement which held the body politic together and prevented both the tyranny of royal authority exercised without consultation and the lawless chaos which sets in when seigneurs are independent of royal control. The direct relationship between these early *placita* and the later *parlement* is a thesis on which he pronounced with caution: "Here, as I see it, is the primitive origin and institution of the *parlements;* they were not, of course, formed all at once in their permanent shape; they evolved rather according to the different times, and under the Capetians they assumed new shapes."[40] In a second, much longer essay, he traces the history of the *parlement* from the time when documentary evidence is available. He shows how the growing needs of royal justice caused Philip the Fair to establish regular meetings of his law officers in 1302, and how these courts became specialized in their functions when, beginning in the reign of Charles VI, the *parlement* began to function permanently. He quotes the rele-

[40] *Ibid.*, p. 76.

vant edicts, ordinances, and royal charters and describes the
composition of the courts and the salary of the royal officers.
He explains the social changes which occurred in the composition of the *parlement*'s officers; when the *parlement* begins to be
held permanently, the "seigneurs suivans les armes" could no
longer sit in it and their place was taken up entirely by "gens
de robe longue."[41]

Pasquier stays very close to his sources: the official acts of
the fourteenth-century monarchy and the registers of the *parlement*. He quotes at great length from the best texts he can find.
His essay is much more than a collection of sources for the
history of the *parlement*, for he always poses the important
questions and then proceeds to what he calls his "demonstrations oculaires," printing the texts so that his readers can touch
these matters "with their fingers."

Perhaps the most remarkable feature of Pasquier's historical
method is the boundless variety of his sources. Everything is
grist to his mill: an act of *parlement*, a papal bull, a poem, a
coin, a statue, the record of a trial, a chronicle; all authentic
remains, if possible contemporary with the event in question,
can supply testimony. To prove that as late as 1380 there were
still noblemen in the law courts, he points to the evidence of
the funeral statue standing in the Church of St. Etienne des
Grecs, whose inscription reads "Messire Pierre de la Neu-ville,
Chevalier Seigneur de Mourray & iadis Conseiller du Roy nostre
Sire en son Parlement." To prove that the mariner's compass
was known much earlier than most people thought, he puts his
unequalled knowledge of French medieval literature at the service of his interest in the history of technology and discovers
documentary proof, in a twelfth-century poem, of the use of
the mariner's compass.[42] But it was not surprising that the

41 *Ibid.*, pp. 80–99.

42 The fourteenth-century epitaph is quoted in *Recherches,* p. 81, and the
twelfth-century poem (Hugues de Berzé's continuation of the *Bible Guyot*),
ibid., p. 625. This is still the earliest known description of the mariner's
compass.

sources he uses most frequently and to best advantage are legal sources and, among them, especially the registers of the *parlement* of Paris.

It is natural, therefore, that Pasquier should be at his best when his researches lead him into the fourteenth and fifteenth centuries. There the documentation is most abundant, it becomes easier to control one text with another, and the issues are both of greater importance and closer to Pasquier's own world. Consequently Pasquier's faults as a historian are less apparent here: his maniacal need to explain, which doesn't always cease when the evidence ceases, and his impatience with detail. Because of the abundant sources available for the later centuries, there is less need for speculation to bridge the gaps between evidence; and because the subject of the fall and rise of France during the Hundred Years' War is of the utmost importance to him, he is more careful in his handling of details.

The Hundred Years' War

Pasquier treats this subject in three long consecutive essays.[43] The first is all tragedy: the disintegration of France under Charles VI; the second restores the balance: Charles VII puts the state back on its feet; the third is devoted to Joan of Arc. In all three of these essays Pasquier succeeds so admirably in cutting short the chroniclers, in extracting the marrow from the bone as his favorite, Rabelais, would have said, in constructing a brisk and clear narrative out of the confusion of partisan accounts that his essays, with minor corrections, could still serve as an excellent introduction to this period.

In the first essay he begins by explaining that it is necessary to go back to the first origins of the civil disorders because of the extreme importance of this subject. Its importance lies, of course, in its similarity to the *troubles* which were disrupting France in Pasquier's generation. He wishes his contemporaries

---

[43] *Ibid.*, pp. 677–719.

could learn how to handle the difficulties of their own time from his analysis of the troubles of the last century, but this is clearly only a pious hope: "Let us hope that, God willing, these [disasters] will teach us something and that we will become wise, in the middle of our own civil disorders, by learning from the mistakes of our ancestors."

In a few sentences he sketches the beginning of the king's madness in 1392. This was the cause of the disorders which followed. For the Princes of the Blood saw their opportunity in the king's weakness. The first strike of the princes was against the king's officers, the financial specialists whose policies had strengthened royal power and brought on the hatred not only of the nobility but also of the common people who suffered from the heavy burden of taxation. Having ousted these men from the court, the princes' intrigues grew in scope, but there was no one to intrigue against except each other. Thus, the duke of Orléans took over the finances of the kingdom, provoking the hatred of the other princes, especially that of his uncle, Philip of Burgundy; he also debased the coinage and imposed a new extraordinary *taille* on the people. In his foreign policy he attempted a rapprochement with Avignon against whose authority both the *parlement* and the university had pronounced themselves. He alienated the *grands* of the nobility by refusing to share his power with them, the common people by imposing new taxes, and the university and the French clergy by his papal diplomacy. These mistakes of Orléans gave Burgundy the opportunity to come to power in his turn. Opposing Orléans' policies, he received support from those who had suffered from them. Thus two parties were created in France.

In a few quick sentences Pasquier sums up the dramatic anecdotes with which his sources are filled. The pathos, the bravery, the murder—all these are only superficial symptoms of a disease which is spreading: the suffocation of the state. The contrast between the chronicles and Pasquier's account is striking; where Monstrelet wanders aimlessly from year to year between battles and heralds' speeches, filling hundreds and hundreds of pages,

Pasquier selects, with very precise questions in mind, only the elements of his answer. He is not, for the moment, interested in everything that may have happened in the reign of Charles VI. One can be sure that he is putting away in some file for future reference this or that bit of information, to be checked against other possible sources and to be used some day for some purpose. But for the moment he has only one thing in mind: an analysis of the agony of the state in the course of the mad king's reign. Everything else will have to wait.

He always prefers official records to the accounts of the chroniclers. The records—those of the *parlement*, of the crown, of the provost's office—are terse and to the point: on such and such a day, sentence was rendered in the presence of so and so, the accusations were such, the convictions such. There are no dramatic embellishments. When Pasquier needs information he cannot find in the registers of the courts, he chooses his informants carefully, noting their bias, comparing their stories with conflicting accounts and always following the principle of relying, all other things being equal, on the source closest to the event.

As he traces the party conflict between Burgundians and Armagnacs (the Orléans party), which seems to him the most important thread to follow in narrating the disintegration of royal power in those years, Pasquier manages to retain an almost incredible degree of objectivity. For a man of his convictions, of his position, and of his time, it must have been very difficult not to be anti-Burgundian, especially after the Burgundian alliance with England. But Pasquier uses pro-Burgundian sources like Monstrelet and the Bourgeois of Paris and sets them off with pro-Armagnac writers like Juvenal des Ursins. Both parties are in the wrong: that is the clear point which emerges out of this essay, although Pasquier rarely judges openly. He is narrating a tragic story, that of the death of a state, saved only by a last-minute miracle. He wants to know how it happened.

Still, Pasquier's own views are fairly clear: he is for peace in

the fifteenth century as in his own time. He observes that peace
in the kingdom can be maintained only by strong royal power.
When this is lacking, all the naturally rebellious forces in the
nation are let loose: the feuding nobility, the mobs of the cities,
and the rabble-rousing preachers. Neither Armagnac nor Burgundian, Pasquier's politics are those of a peace-loving, well-
to-do burgher; when the rule of law is challenged by violence
in the streets, when crops are burned and business is at a stand-
still and magistrates are hanged by mobs, when power-hungry
magnates whose only trade-in-stock is war and hysterical monks
who have no stake in this world's order take over from reasonable, educated men, then things are very bad indeed. It was
just such an extremity in which France found herself during
the reign of Charles VI.

Rather than siding with one senseless clique or another, Pasquier tries to distinguish from among the mass of demented
who drove the country to its ruin the few reasonable men who
stood up for law and order. If there is a hero in the small camp
of the latter, it is Master Juvenal des Ursins, a prominent Parisian bourgeois, once provost of the merchants, who, at the time
of the crisis, held the office of *avocat du roy* at the *parlement*.
He was the only *homme de robe longue* who dared to champion
the cause of peace. The simple fact that Pasquier allows Master
Juvenal several pages in which to show his brave and competent handling of mobs and courtiers, while the battle of Agincourt does not quite take up a single sentence in the same essay,
shows that Pasquier exercises a selectivity which is dictated not
only by the availability of reliable sources—these were available in both cases—but also by a philosophical perspective in
which battles are unimportant and virtuous magistrates are
heroes.

From somber intrigue to bloody murder, Pasquier follows
the fortunes of France to their lowest point, when Philip of Burgundy openly "se fit Anglois" in 1419, after his father's murder
at Montereau. In the next essay he begins at the point when all
seems lost and France is almost absorbed by the English, but

somehow, as if by miracle, salvation is at hand—by miracle, because the dauphin Charles was hardly "un subject capable pour cest effect."

How, then, was the recovery of France effected? While the dauphin, a vicious imbecile as Pasquier presents him, was playing games with his ladies, the English almost conquered France. But God had mercy on the French and provided the king with some first-rate generals who stopped the luck of the English in 1426 at the siege of Montargis. Two years later Joan of Arc arrived. Her propaganda and her military leadership brought on a torrent of victories and culminated in the coronation at Reims. Unfortunately Joan was wounded in an attack on Paris and her luck changed; she was captured and executed. But the power of the English in France was already declining, as can be seen from the audacity of the *parlement* of Paris, which went on strike for higher wages. The English lost one battle after another. How was their power broken? In the concluding sentence of this essay, Pasquier sums up his answer: "As I have already said at the beginning of this chapter, there was something miraculous about the restoration of the affairs of France. . . . God sent her good and loyal generals in her extremity and even our Pucelle: But it would have been an even greater miracle if Henry V, after conquering most of France, had been able to transmit his conquest to his children, leaving, as he did, at his death, an infant of only 16 months to succeed him at the head of the state. . . ." The conclusion is clear: France was saved by the death of Henry V and by the ability of her generals. Miracles really had nothing to do with it. There is no talk of France's destiny here, no ill feeling toward the English, and no mystique about Joan of Arc. A dispassionate social scientist notes the accident of a royal death and the accident of capable generals: given these, it would have taken a miracle for things to have turned out other than they did.

Pasquier's treatment of the *affaire* Joan of Arc is restrained and sober. Not that he underestimates the part played by the *pucelle* in the defeat of the English; but he does not portray her as a saint on horseback or the incarnation of France. He notes the mystical fervor kindled by the girl among the common people of France, a fervor which outlasted Joan's short lifetime; but for him she remains a human being, a poor girl who was intimidated, tortured, and defamed by her contemporaries and by posterity.

The legend of Joan of Arc was never systematically developed before the French Revolution. She was hardly given any part to play in the more or less official histories of France composed by Gilles, Gaguin, Emilio, or Vignier. When historians did tell her story, they were most likely intent on debunking the folk tales and offered, as did Du Haillan, a super-rationalist version in which Joan appears as a clever whore manipulated by courtiers. These speculations, just like the legendary tales of her miracles, were founded on oral tradition and on literary sources of late and dubious origin. Meanwhile there were first-rate sources available for the history of Joan of Arc, namely the records of the trial proceedings. Yet, Pasquier is almost alone in going to these records and founding his account on a critical study of the trials.[44]

Pasquier's essay on Joan of Arc is a model of scholarship and exposition.[45] He begins with an introduction in which he gives the historiographical dossier of the problem, presents his own thesis, and explains his documentation. The existing historiography on Joan of Arc is hostile. Pasquier distinguishes three schools: English or Burgundian sympathizers, for whom she is an enemy; the Machiavellian rationalists, for whom Joan is nothing but a successful propaganda trick devised by Charles' ministers; and finally, those who claim that she was a talented slut who had been sleeping with Baudricourt and others at court before her crafty masters gave her the assignment of pretending to hear voices and began to arrange miracles for her, such as

---

[44] See Robert Hanhart, *Das Bild der Jeanne d'Arc in der französischen Historiographie vom Spätmittelalter bis zur Aufklärung* (Basel, 1955). Above all, consult Appendix III *post*.

[45] Pasquier, *Recherches*, pp. 708–719.

the famous scene in which she picks out the dauphin from among his entourage.

Pasquier can understand the English burning her; he can even understand the Machiavellians, who are, after all, only being fashionable; but with those who slander her memory he has no patience, because this slander is directed not only against the girl herself but against France: was it a lying slut who saved the country and crowned the king at Reims?

Pasquier does not waste time being indignant. He simply points out that his own conclusions are based on solid evidence: the records of the trial proceedings, which he has had in his possession during a period of four years. He proceeds to give his version of Joan's trial, following the documents very closely, quoting frequently and remaining critical throughout. In eleven pages of narrative he succeeds in giving a succinct and faithful picture of the trial; the essence is all there and he misses nothing of the simple drama of Joan's responses to the judges. He manages to include all the principal questions and answers and at the same time to exclude the judicial red tape and theological claptrap with which the proceedings were burdened. What he gives his readers in this short essay is exactly what he promises, "the soul of the trial."

Having done this he returns to the original question: was Joan a hypocrite, a dupe, or an inspired virgin? The question revolves around her voices: did she really hear them? The evidence of the trials, Pasquier concludes, can only lead to one answer: for if it could be argued that Joan's voices were a trick at the time of her arrival at court (characteristically, Pasquier admits that he cannot come to a conclusion on this question for lack of evidence), this argument falls down as one examines the trial records. Now that she was in the hands of the law, she refused to give up her clothes, after a momentary weakness, even though she knew that the consequence of her refusal would be a cruel death. What made her so obstinate in her refusal? What possible interest could prevail against the fear of death and torture? One could only believe the answer she herself gave to her judges: she was obeying her voices. "What conclusion can one reach then, about Joan, if one is to speak without passion? Only one conclusion is possible: that she believes that all these voices came from God."

Philosophy of history

The reader who has followed Pasquier's *demonstrations oculaires* will be tempted to put his success down to his knowledge of sources and to his practical method as a historian. If Pasquier is an innovator, one might argue, it is because he goes to the archives instead of contenting himself with narrative sources of dubious value. There lies Pasquier's originality, not in his philosophy which is "judiciously banal."[46]

To be sure, Pasquier's historical criticism, when he is at his best, is entirely modern. On the other hand, his rare philosophical statements seem to remain entirely within the bounds of classical and Christian convention.[47] The student of sixteenth-century historical scholarship, however, is not surprised to find competent textual criticism in the *Recherches*; the contrary would be surprising in a book written by a *parlementaire* trained in the tradition of the *mos Gallicus*. There are many scholars of Pasquier's caliber among his contemporaries. The techniques of historical investigation are developed, the collection and edition of texts proceed at a rapid pace in the sixteenth century, and this flow of erudition will continue, uninterrupted, to the present day, although the seventeenth-century continuators are often less capable than the great masters of Pasquier's generation.

46 This is the conclusion of Bouteiller in the only modern article devoted to Pasquier's historical method, "E. Pasquier."

47 So much so that a Swiss divinity student argues in his doctoral thesis that Pasquier's philosophy was nothing more than conventional Christian moralism. See Bütler, *Nationales und universales Denken im Werke E. Pasquiers*.

In the context of this general movement of erudition, it is not Pasquier's techniques as such that distinguish his work from that of his contemporaries. The documents concerning the trial of Joan of Arc were available to scholars: Pasquier saw them in the libraries of St. Victor and Fontainebleau. There is no problem of technical skill here; any number of his colleagues could have read these legal documents. But Pasquier knew what to do with them, as he knew what to do with Caesar's memoirs. Everywhere, always, Pasquier has a point of view. That is precisely what most of his contemporaries lack.

If historians had no philosophy in the 1560s, it was not for lack of trying. Nothing shows more clearly the great need for a philosophical approach to the past than the proliferation of learned treatises on historical method, the *artes historicae*.[48] The great bulk of these only repeated the commonplaces of classical rhetoric on the subject of history: history is the teacher of life and the historian an impartial judge collecting *exempla* for posterity; history is considered a branch of rhetoric, the historian an observer, his subject politics. These treatises described history as it was written by the Romans.[49]

Of these formal discourses on history, only two were relevant to the problems of historical study facing Pasquier, those written by the French jurists Baudouin and Bodin a few years after the publication of the first book of the *Recherches*.[50] Baudouin and Bodin drew the conclusions for historiography of the teaching of the *mos Gallicus*. Tinged with Protestantism and French nationalism, their works were attempts to erect a scientific

[48] On the *artes historicae* as a genre, see Brown, *"Methodus" of Jean Bodin*, and Beatrice Reynolds, "Shifting Currents in Historical Criticism," *Journal of the History of Ideas* 14 (1939), pp. 471–492.

[49] See George H. Nadel, "Philosophy of History before Historicism," *History and Theory* 2 (1964), pp. 291–315.

[50] Jean Bodin, *Methodus ad facilem historiarum cognitionem* (Paris, 1566) and François Baudouin, *De institutione historiae et eius cum jurisprudentia conjunctione* (Paris, 1561).

system on the foundation of historical jurisprudence. The application of the methods of the *mos Gallicus* to all historical problems, they agreed, would eventually produce firm criteria for distinguishing good laws from bad ones and good institutions from bad ones. The scientific analysis of the past would put an end to all the confusions and contradictions of the present since each course of action would become indisputably clear for the lawyer as well as for the statesman. Kings and prelates, informed by history, would act rightly. Even the future would eventually be predicted.

While Pasquier respected Baudouin and Bodin and was generally sympathetic with their views, he was too much the practicing historian, too much the lover of facts, to be attracted by their positivism. He, too, was confident in the historical method, but he was aware of the difficulties as no theorist could be. The subjectivity of historical knowledge, the great gaps in documentation, the difficulty of reaching firm conclusions in his investigations, these prevented him from embracing the boundless optimism of the theorists. As much as he loved to explain, he stopped short of explaining away in the grand manner of Bodin. He could not convince himself that the climate or the stars governed the destiny of nations. As for the traditional Christian view, he implicitly ignored it in his work. Pasquier does not for a moment believe that the course of human history is to be understood as a long fall from grace. On this question, he would agree with Bodin, for whom history was the progress of humanity from savagery to civilization, the highest stage of which, so far, had been reached by men in his own century. Pasquier is a good Christian, but his historiography is secular.

Although conventional statements about Fortune and divine providence are to be found in the *Recherches*, they serve no functional purpose. Sometimes they are simply the product of habit, a pure reflex, a manner of speaking, clichés unavoidable in a man of Pasquier's upbringing. Sometimes Pasquier uses these phrases as a smokescreen behind which he can hide from his traditionalist critics. At other times, such statements appear in a downright subversive context, as is the case in the essay on Joan of Arc. Pasquier's Jesuit critics will not miss the point: they brand him a libertine.[51]

Pasquier would not deny that men can, in principle, learn from the mistakes of the past; he has no thought of denying, in principle, that God's will is the motive force behind human history. These two contradictory assumptions, the commonplaces of historical philosophy in his day, simply serve no purpose in his work. They are there as a reassuring façade just barely thick enough to hide the truly radical implications of his researches.

Implications, that is all they are. Pasquier does not build a philosophical system, nor does he directly challenge traditional views. The philosophy of history which informs his researches remains nameless, incomplete and unrecognized even by his most malicious critics, who can do no more than compile a catalogue of heresies. This catalogue, however, is an index to a coherent philosophy of history.

Pasquier is philosophical in two distinct ways: in the way he thinks about his work as an historian and in the way he thinks about the subject of his researches, France. The fundamental question he must ask himself about his work is that of the skeptics: is it possible at all to find out what happened in the past? His life's work is an affirmative answer to this question, and yet this affirmation is hedged with many serious doubts. There are certainly historical problems which cannot be solved at all, for lack of documentation. The earliest centuries of French history are lost to the historian for all practical purposes. Here, where there are so few reliable sources, one has to proceed in the dark (*à tastons*) and one can only guess at what happened. It is not easy for Pasquier to resign himself to this immense loss.

[51] Garasse, *Recherches*, pp. 681ff.

Another obstacle in the way of historical knowledge is the subjectivity of the historian's perception of events:

> For History, as you know, is a very ticklish business. Its principal purpose being the discovery of truth, the historian necessarily writes down hearsay evidence, unless he was himself an eyewitness to the events. If it is hearsay, you know how little one can trust the reports of others and how everyone presents things so as to make his own party look good. If the historian was an eyewitness, we need only remember how, when a town is taken, each of the inhabitants speaks differently of the events of the siege, for it is impossible to be present on all sides at once during the attack. In addition, if you write of your own time, you have to flatter your Prince, to whom you owe more loyalty, or whom you fear.

Finally, stronger than all other biases is the historian's religious belief. Even in a supremely honest historian like Sleidan, who surmounts most other obstacles to objectivity, "you will notice *ie ne sçay quoy de passion*, when he touches upon matters which involve his religion."[52]

Even under the best conditions, when documentation is available and bias under control, Pasquier does not consider the results of the historian's research definitive. He is perfectly willing to have them questioned by competent colleagues and revised, if necessary. Vignier and Pithou, among others, corrected his conclusions on several occasions, "and I can tell you," Pasquier commented, "that I am no less satisfied at being corrected in this manner than when I was highly praised by them."[53]

History may be a "very ticklish business" and it may be very difficult to be a historian without "falsifying the truth," but Pasquier never lets himself fall into the pyrrhonistic anxieties of La Popelinière or the hypercriticism of Vignier, in the face

---

[52] Pasquier, "Pourparler du Prince," *Recherches*, pp. 1130–31.

[53] Pasquier, *Lettres,* p. 244. Compare with Vignier's statement quoted above, Chap. 2, note 37.

of the difficulties raised by historical research. The reason for
this, at least in part, is that Pasquier avoids the worst difficulties:
he writes neither universal nor contemporary history. Nor does
he really write the history of France, in the accepted sense of a
continuous narrative. The *Recherches* are a collection of essays
whose arrangement is neither entirely topical nor quite chronological. Each essay owes its existence to some documents which
have come to the author's attention. Pasquier never puts himself
in the awkward position of having to write on some subject for
which reliable sources are not available, because he does not
accept the obligation to construct a continuous narrative in
the classical manner. The sources give his essays not only their
substance but also to some extent their shape. As a result the
book, as it grows over the years, may lack the neat outlines of
the histories advocated by humanist theorists, "but who is to
say" replies Pasquier to this criticism, "that a meadow sprinkled
with all kinds of flowers produced by Nature, without order,
is less pleasing to the eye than flowerbeds artistically arranged
by gardeners?"

Pasquier thinks of his essays as growing naturally, like wild
flowers. This does not mean that their growth is haphazard or
casual; the laws of nature are far more rigorous than the rules
of gardeners. There is nothing accidental about his choice of
topics for research, and nothing accidental about the outline
of the *Recherches*, which is already clearly formed in 1560
although the book will keep growing for sixty-five years. As for
the essays, the first condition for their inclusion in the *Recherches* is that reliable sources should be available for a given
topic, but among all the topics for which such documentation
exists, Pasquier selects some and ignores others. What is the
principle of selection?

He ignores military and diplomatic history, despite the great
abundance of sources in these fields. He prefers to hunt down
out-of-the-way evidence in order to pursue the topic that really
interests him, the internal evolution of French society. The
medieval chroniclers, of course, never wrote with this interest

in mind, which makes Pasquier's task more difficult.[54] A good example of his method is his treatment of the Crusades. Despite the voluminous materials available to him for writing a history of these voyages and of the conquests overseas, Pasquier ignores the voyages as such in his essay. His question is this: "What benefits did we draw from the overseas voyages which our ancestors called crusades?" He answers this question by analyzing the effect of the Crusades on French society: because many powerful feudal magnates left France, King Philip and his successor Louis were able to tame the lesser nobles and restore royal authority.[55] Evidently, Pasquier imposes his demands on the sources before he lets them shape his history. In this instance, as always, Pasquier subordinates the data, even when he trusts them, to the overall purpose of his researches.

The purpose is clear: it is to define France. France is not a territory and it is not a dynastic possession: it is a perpetually changing concept which can only be defined through its history. The Celts who inhabited Gaul centuries before Christ and Caesar, whose language, whose laws, whose religion were so radically different from those of his contemporaries, were already French by virtue of the vestiges of their customs still embedded in French society and culture. Continuity as well as change were constantly operating to maintain what was distinctly French: the laws, the customs, and the language of the people.

The success of a battle, the death of a king, even a change of

---

[54] ". . . qui est celuy (ie n'en excepteray aucun) qui, apres avoir quelque peu sauté sur les guerres, nous ait iamais discouru le faict de nostre police?" Pasquier, *Recherches*, p. 7.

[55] "Nostre France estant par le moyen de ce voyage espuisee d'une bonne partie des grands . . . desquels les petits se targeoient contre l'autorité de nos Rois, le Roy Philippes, & Louys le Gros son fils commencerent de les harasser, ou pour mieux dire terrasser: & specialement Louys surmonta un Hugue, sieur de Puissay en Beausse, Boucard Seigneur de Montmorēcy, Milles Comte de Mõtlehery, Eude Comte de Corbeil, Guy Comte de Rochefort, Thomas Comte de Merles. A l'excēple desquels tous les autres communs Seigneurs se reduisirent souz la totale obeissance de nos Rois." *Ibid.*, p. 777 (incorrectly numbered 773).

dynasty were only outward symptoms of this organic process. The Gauls were conquered not by the accident of a military campaign but because their institutions were at fault. The success of the French kingdom since the Frankish conquest, on the other hand, was due to the judicious grafting of Roman, Christian, and Germanic elements onto the original Celtic institutions. In this perspective events such as the battle of Agincourt or even the Crusades, which may have seemed momentous to the chroniclers, are reduced to mere outward effects caused by deeper strengths and weaknesses in French society. The nation, as Pasquier understands it, is an entity distinct from the state and distinct from race. The nation is defined by its customs, its laws, and its culture: these form a unique and dynamic structure of which the state is merely an expression and which can absorb conquering races.

Pasquier's historicist definition of the French nation must be understood in the context of the sixteenth-century intellectual movement which gave it birth and not as a forerunner of nineteenth-century ideologies. It had been elaborated by the masters of the *mos Gallicus* in the course of their study of Roman institutions. These humanist jurists, of necessity, could not treat Rome as a state or as a race, since Rome's laws, its language, and its culture transcended its political or racial existence. Roman institutions survived the end of the empire, exercised by Germans and Greeks. Cujas and his disciples perceived Rome as a civilization and developed a historical method for the study of civilizations. This concept and this method served as Pasquier's model for the study of France.

French civilization, from the first page of the *Recherches* to the last, is defined by contrast with Roman civilization. Urged on by the desire to prove that France possesses all the attributes of a civilization, that, like Rome, it has a long history, a high culture, a coherent body of laws and institutions, Pasquier ends up praising the differences between France and Rome. French poetry, French architecture, and French law are not only comparable to the products of Roman civilization,

but they are superior in the sense that they are alive and growing. He grants that this was not always so; when Gaul was a
province of the empire, Roman laws were better and were
rightly borrowed by the Gauls. That was a long time ago, and
since then the French have developed their own law and no
longer need to borrow from the Romans.[56]

Born of the comparison between Rome and France, Pasquier's historicism eventually extended to all things; he could
not watch his children play without plunging into the history
of children's games. In his last years he became more and more
interested in the Bible and in religious questions in general. As
he read the New Testament, he could not help applying the
historical method to this document also. He began to worry
about the value of the four gospel narratives as primary sources
(why do they all jump from the Nativity to Jesus' twenty-ninth
or thirtieth year?) and about their relation to each other.[57]

His views on Protestantism were also the product of his
fundamental historicism. The Reformation is a phenomenon
which can only be explained through its history. As a Catholic,
he concedes that Luther's heresy "ought to be detested," but
in the next sentence he declares he is convinced that Pope Leo
was "the first and principal instrument of this divorce," an idea
that would seem to exonerate Luther. Not that Leo is to blame
either; from his point of view it seemed right to announce a
crusade against the Turkish menace and to raise funds for this
purpose. Yet, when the danger was past the selling of indulgences should have been stopped. On the other hand, it was

---

[56] "Toutes les Provinces anciennement qui estoient subjettes a l'Empire,
avoient, comme il est vraysemblable, diversement leurs loix municipales:
en quoy si elles manquoient en quelque cas, qui n'eust esté definy, c'estoit
bien la raison que les Provinciaux eussent recours, en l'obmission de tels
cas, au droit commun de l'Empire, sous lequel ils estoient assubjettis: mais
de nous chaulser à ce mesme poinct, ce seroit faire tort à nostre patrie."
Pasquier, *Lettres*, p. 225.

[57] *Ibid.*, pp. 611–614.

perfectly reasonable for Luther to preach against this abuse, and the Pope should have heeded the warning and disavowed the indulgence sellers. Luther would have desisted and the break within the Church could have been avoided.[58] The Protestant revolt, then, was simply produced like everything else, by the actions of men.

Pasquier's historicism keeps him from seeing the Reformation as the work of Satan; it also keeps him from embracing Protestantism. Although he is fully aware of the faults of the Roman church and although he hopes for its reformation, he argues the case against Protestantism on historical grounds (*Je diray seulement ce que je pense estre de l'histoire*) without entering the domain of the theologians (*Je ne fais poinct profession de Theologie*). His case is this: the evidence of the texts shows that most of the ceremonies and propositions attacked by the Protestants were in fact practiced by the time of Tertullian. These "idolatries," then, far from being momentary aberrations, have been part of the church for a very long time. Pasquier refuses to believe that God left all Christians in error during all these centuries. The long historical existence of these beliefs justifies them in Pasquier's eyes.[59]

His reasoning leads him inevitably to relativism, and he does not shrink from it when he is speaking in general terms or when the issues are far enough from his own concerns. Laws, customs, and religious ceremonies are the product of history. As such they are different in different regions and at different times. The burial customs of the Indians horrified the Greeks and vice versa.[60] Presumably, then, there is no way to prove that one custom is better than another.

Yet this is where Pasquier starts cheating. He has some very definite notions about good customs, just laws, and right action,

[58] *Ibid.*, pp. 607–610.
[59] *Ibid.*, p. 266.
[60] *Ibid.*, p. 267.

but when the historical relativism to which he subscribes in principle leads him to conclusions which he finds personally unacceptable, he invokes utility and, failing that, reason. Why, for instance, should heresy not be rooted out with sword and fire? There certainly is enough historical precedent for such an action, cruel and barbarous though it may be. Pasquier abhors violence and cherishes the freedom to think, but he cannot argue against religious fanaticism on these grounds. Instead, he claims that violence has not, in the past, proved an effective method for the suppression of heresy.

Here we have a clue, easy to follow up even without Father Garasse's garrulous compendium, to Pasquier's libertinism. The Jesuit's definition of libertinism approximates the meaning given to the terms "enlightened" or "philosophical" in the eighteenth century. If one discounts the exaggerations of this caricature and simply takes Pasquier as he presents himself in his essays and in his letters, the portrait which emerges is that of an Erasmian humanist.

Pasquier likes the Stoics. He likes Erasmus—and also Rabelais and Montaigne. But he is a man of action: no library in a tower, no *abbaye de Thélème* for him. He is attracted by the notion of retiring to his country house and giving himself up entirely to the pleasures of contemplation and discourse with his friends, but, despite some nostalgic twinges for this secularized monastic ideal, he leans toward the ideal of the active life, that of the engaged intellectual who is as common in his time as in Voltaire's. The *Recherches* and the letters are marked on every page by Pasquier's activism, that is, by the political maxims embodied in the *demonstrations* he wishes his readers to "touch with their fingers," and toward which all his researches inexorably gravitate.

Outstanding among these are the virtues, historically demonstrated, of peace, national unity, religious toleration, learning, and economic prosperity. Founded on the New Testament and on the Stoics, eminently bourgeois and anti-clerical, humanist and humane, Pasquier's philosophy stands somewhere between Erasmus and Voltaire in the history of liberalism. With these great men, Pasquier shares a superb confidence in the virtues of learning and reason, and little confidence in the common man's ability to achieve these.

Nonetheless, the bitterness, the sarcasm, and the complaints found so often in the writings of humanist liberals and their frequent longings for the virtues of distant lands and distant heroes are absent in Pasquier, perhaps because he had better opportunities for influencing events than most intellectuals have, at least in their lifetime. No *Lumpenproletarier*, Pasquier was born into modest wealth and respectable social position. In the 1540s and 1550s he studied classical philology and law with the most famous professors in Europe at a time when these disciplines were surrounded with an aura of exclusiveness comparable to that surrounding nuclear physics today. As a member everywhere of the leading academic clique, Pasquier formed lifelong friendships with the most capable French scholars of his age. As a young man he dabbled in poetry, enough to participate in the most fashionable literary *salons* and to befriend men like Ronsard and Du Bellay. He was perhaps a scholar among the poets and a poet among the scholars. In any case he moved freely from one constituency of the Republic of Letters to another. He knew the poets, the historians, the theologians, the jurists, the antiquarians, the painters, architects, and musicians, the physicians and other men of science. He was not only a universal observer in the world of culture, he also performed important political functions as a royal officer in the *parlement*. He played politics as a stalwart of the *politique* party and saw all his hopes for France realized by the accession of Henri IV and later shattered by his assassination.

After the king's murder, Pasquier turned toward Biblical criticism and kept working on the last book of the *Recherches*, a history of universities. His correspondence became more limited in scope, since most of his old friends were dead, but he kept up his régime of research and letter writing and he supervised the education of his grandchildren.

The life Pasquier led as a magistrate during the civil wars, the education he received, the friendships he cultivated, and the way of life he kept up in his Paris townhouse and in his country house near Fontainebleau, all these belong to a very definite world, the charmed circle of well-to-do intellectuals which flourished in France during the sixteenth century. This social set was solidly founded on the money, the leisure, and the culture of the *haute bourgeoisie*. Still, money and social position were not absolute requirements in this world where self-made men like Bodin were esteemed as much as members of the establishment like De Thou. In the rich and earnest setting of the magisterial houses, men and even, occasionally, women of the most diverse backgrounds met on the common ground of their interests in classical literature, law, art, history, mathematics, science, philology, and philosophy.

The tone of these *salons* was pedantic and encyclopaedic. Despite real differences among those who frequented them, these earnest meetings had a general political and philosophical point of view as distinct, perhaps, if not as loudly proclaimed, as that of the eighteenth-century *salons* frequented by the *philosophes*.

When enough is known about the world of the late Renaissance intellectuals in Paris, the *Recherches* will be much better understood. For the moment, one has to be content to note that aside from the historicism and the nationalism in Pasquier's thought, there is a third element which could provisionally be called Erasmian. The study of Roman law taught Pasquier that civilizations are both different from each other and comparable, and that they change in time. As a patriotic Frenchman living at a time when the political existence of his country was threatened, he was impelled to choose France as the focus of his researches and thus discovered a modern historical perspective. This kind of legal study and this kind of patriotism remained essentially limited in France to what I should call the *culture de robe*. Here Pasquier found not only a new method and a new purpose for historical research but also a new point of view, almost an ideology, which enabled him to transform antiquarian studies into philosophical history.

The origins of the nation

Fourth chapter

The heroes of the Trojan war who figured so prominently in the pedigrees of ancient nations continued to perform the function of mythical sires for the new nations of medieval Europe. The Franks especially, from the time of the Merovingian kings, filled the darkest recesses of their forgotten past with elaborate fictions of ancient Trojan splendor. In a seventh-

This chapter was originally published in a considerably different version under the title "The Trojan Franks and Their Critics" in *Studies in the Renaissance* 12 (1965), pp. 227–241.

century chronicle Priam appears as the first king of the Franks.[1] After the fall of Troy, according to the Merovingian chronicler, some Trojans escaped the disaster and elected a man named Francio king.[2] Francio's people, after a long and warlike exodus, eventually materialized over the Rhine as the Franks who invaded Gaul.

The adoption of Trojan paternity was a common enough device for the regularization of a new nation's status.[3] The Trojan pedigree was glorious and ancient; it established one's blood relationship with the Romans, and it justified one's title to the possession of parts of the Roman empire. Thus, from the start of its thousand-year-long career, this myth was to be the property of the state as well as a theme for poets. The Trojan origins of the French remained an article of faith for the monarchy. As late as 1714, the learned Nicolas Fréret was thrown into the Bastille for showing that the Franks were Germans.[4]

To be sure, the Valois and Bourbon kings had reasons for affirming their Trojan ancestry which were different from the motives of the Merovingians. It was no longer necessary to justify the Frankish conquest of Gaul and to rest one's claim on an elective affinity with the Romans. The needs of royal propaganda were of a different order in the sixteenth century

---

[1] "Exinde origo Francorum fuit. Priamo primo regi habuerant. . . ." *Chronicarum quae dicuntur Fredegarii Scholastici libri IV cum continuationibus*, ed. B. Krusch (1888), *Monumenta Germaniae historica*, Scriptorum rerum Merovingicarum, II, p. 45. On the continuous medieval tradition and its many versions see Maria Klippel, *Die Darstellung der fränkischen Trojanersage* (Marburg, 1936). A. Joly in *Benoit de Sainte-More et le roman de Troie* (Paris, 1871), p. 122, suggested that the story of their Trojan origin must have been well established and endowed with official sanction among the Franks by the time this chronicle was composed. He quotes (without giving a specific reference, however) a charter of King Dagobert in which one reads that the Franks were "ex nobilissimo et antiquo Trojanorum reliquarium sanguine nati."

[2] Fredegarius, *Chronicarum*, p. 46.

[3] See Denys Hay, *Europe: The Emergence of an Idea* (Edinburgh, 1957), p. 49, on the widespread use of the Trojan myth by European nations. See also Joly, *Benoit de Ste.-More*, p. 118.

[4] On Fréret, see the article "Fréret" in *Larousse du XIXe siècle*.

and later.[5] The new purpose was to deny that the Franks were
a Germanic people. Sycophantic historians writing for the
seventeenth-century court could even go so far on occasion as
to deny the Trojan origin if only they made it clear that the
Franks were not Germans either.[6]

Presumably, then, and this has been the consensus of modern
scholarship until now, the Trojan myth was not clearly rejected
and replaced by a scientific explanation of Frankish origins
before the eighteenth century.[7] There may have been doubts,
even openly expressed criticism of the Trojan story at an earlier
date, but political pressure and the limitations of early modern
historical criticism prevented the eradication of the legend and
the substitution for it of a scientific account. This was the view
expressed by A. Joly in his fine book on the *roman de Troie*,[8]
while Denys Hay, like Joly, observed in a recent book that the
learned were growing hostile to the Trojan legend by the second
half of the sixteenth century and concluded that the real influence of the legend on historians was over by about 1600,
even though the Trojans were still orthodox in the seventeenth
century.[9]

5 On this, see Vittorio de Caprariis, *Propaganda e pensiero politico in
Francia durante le guerre di religione* (Naples, 1959).

6 "Encore que ie face sortir les François de Vesfalie, de Frise, de Saxe, de
Turinge, de Hesse & de Misnie Province de Germanie, & des terres arrousees
des rivieres, Oemis, Elbe, Lippe, Isel, Vater, Veser, Adrana, Nexer, Meyor &
du Rhin, fleuves d'Allemagne. Ie n'avouë pas neãtmoins qu'ils en fussent
originaires; ie dis que les peuples appelez Francs estoiët une colonie sortie
des Gaules. . . ." Father Jean-Estienne Taraut, *Annales de France* (Paris,
1635), p. 58.

7 See, for instance, Lot: "Ce fut une stupeur indignée quand Fréret, à la fin
du siècle de Louis XIV, osa prêtendre que les Francs étaient un peuple
germanique. . . . Jusqu'alors les personnes savantes, utilisant les fabrications
naives de clercs, remontant à l'ère mérovingienne finissante, se les repré-
sentaient comme les descendants des Troyens. . . ." *La Gaule*, p. 7.

8 "Ainsi la légende troyenne était en pleine déroute a la fin du XVIe siecle,
mais ce n'était pas encore l'histoire vraie qui devait regagner tout de suite
le terrain perdu par elle; la légende hebraique crée par Annius de Viterbo
allait encore quelque temps garder la place." Joly, *Benoit de Ste.-More*, p.
609.

9 Hay, *Europe*, p. 109.

Underlying these casual observations there is a common-sense assumption of a gradual pattern of progress in the history of historical scholarship paralleling the growth of science and rationalism. Following this assumption, the history of the Trojan idea presents itself as a fairly simple scheme: medieval credulity, growing skepticism in the sixteenth and seventeenth centuries, open doubt in the age of the *philosophes*, and, finally, the solution of the problem by the scientific historians of the nineteenth century.

But this is not what actually happened. In the first place, the legend was completely discredited in the course of the sixteenth century, not only in learned circles but at the French court and in French public opinion. Before 1600 it was replaced by a scientific account of Frankish origins which has not been improved upon since.

In the second place, after 1600 the medieval legend returned as the official version in the history books, and the work of historical criticism accomplished in the sixteenth century was often ignored or denounced as impious. Fréret went to jail in 1714 for demonstrating, in the privacy of the meeting room of the Academy of Inscriptions, the same historical theses which in the sixteenth century could be read in the published works of royal historiographers whose books were paid for, dedicated to, and read with interest by Henri III and Henri IV.

At the beginning of the sixteenth century a reader who wished to satisfy his curiosity concerning French antiquity could find the Trojan story in all the annals and chronicles. It was everywhere treated as history and no alternative explanations existed. In Nicole Gilles' *Annales* the medieval tradition was reported straight from the author's sources, the chronicles of St. Denis, Vincent of Beauvais, and Hugh of St. Victor.[10]

For a more sophisticated audience, there was Robert Gaguin's *Compendium de origine et gestis Francorum*. Although Gaguin's approach to his sources does not quite deserve to be

[10] Gilles, *Annales* (Paris, 1525), f. vii, f. viii.

called critical, nevertheless, there is a difference in tone, in emphasis, and in the selection of evidence between his *Compendium* and the *Annales* of Gilles. Even though Gaguin tells the Trojan story on the first page of his history, he reproduces the legend so briefly and with so many qualifications that the reader may conclude that Gaguin himself doubts the story and only presents it reluctantly, through a sense of duty to his sources. He observes that the name of the Franks cannot be found mentioned regularly in any trustworthy author contemporary with their alleged exploits. He also notes that Gregory of Tours, for whom he has great respect, did not know much about the origins of the Franks.[11] These considerations, however, do not lead him to an outright rejection of the legend. He doubted the value of his sources, but he was not capable of systematic criticism. His education and his Italian experience prompted him to abandon fabulous history. On the other hand, he could not carry his doubts to their logical conclusion. Had a better explanation of Frankish origins been available to him, he might have repudiated the old fable.

Gaguin's rival for the position of historiographer at the French court, the Veronese humanist Paolo Emilio, took the next step in his book *De rebus gestis Francorum*. His history, like Gaguin's, opens with a brief account of the traditional view. Then, without bothering to question the sources of the medieval tradition, he calmly quotes Cicero to prove that the Franks were known as a Germanic people in his time.[12] He was wrong,

---

[11] Robert Gaguin, *Compendium de origine et gestis Francorum* (Paris, 1550). The Trojan story is given on f. 1r, but it is followed up on the same page with some qualifications: "Nemo tamen mihi certus auctor lectus est qui tempus eius nominis constanter tradat." And again, "Nec ip̄e gregorius turoneñ gentis initiū satis novit: cum sulpitiū alexandrum testem citet / a quo francorum regum vera origo ignorata videatur." These remarks may have been an afterthought, for they are missing from the 1497 edition.

[12] Emilio, *De rebus gestis* (Paris, 1517), I, f. iii. Cicero wrote of Frangones (ad Att. xiv, 10) by which he meant not a tribal but a family name. See Ludwig Schmidt, *Geschichte der deutschen Stämme* (Berlin, 1904–1918), in *Quellen und Forschungen zur alten Geschichte und Geographie*, ed. W. Sieglin, XXX, p. 433.

of course. Cicero did not know of any Franks; Emilio merely misinterpreted a word. Yet, in a sense he was right too: the Franks were a Germanic people, even if Emilio, having no historical sense and little respect for accuracy, did not know how to prove this hypothesis.[13] His contribution to the progress of historical scholarship was indirect inasmuch as his contempt for the medieval sources led him to wipe out, in a few sentences, centuries of elaborate speculation on the earliest history of the Franks. All he knew (it does not matter that he was wrong) was that Cicero mentioned the Franks. From that time until the fifth century he knew of no reliable sources. On the second page of his book he is already in the year 404, confidently facing an immense void in historical knowledge in preference to the fables Gaguin was still reluctant to part with. His fortitude in this respect was all the more admirable because, while he was ruthlessly pruning the French past of its legends, others were busily creating new ones. Trithemius, a German Benedictine, had only recently "found" eighteen books written by a certain Hunibald, which gave an account of the history of the Franks from the sack of Troy down to the reign of Clovis.[14]

The first probe into the *terra incognita* created by Emilio came from the German humanist Beatus Rhenanus, who started with Emilio's undemonstrated conclusion as a working hypothesis and went on to prove the Franks' Germanic origin.[15]

---

[13] Davies, however, makes the point that the MS drafts of Emilio's history reveal him ". . . as a scholar of wide interests and more conscientious diligence than could be proved from the De Rebus Gestis. . . ." "Late XVth Century French Historiography," p. 171.

[14] For a detailed discussion of these new forgeries, see Joly, *Benoit de Ste.-More,* pp. 550ff.

[15] Beatus Rhenanus, *Rerum Germanicorum libri tres* (Basel, Froben, 1531). The Franks are discussed on pp. 27–39 and 106–108 of this work. A. Du Chesne, in his *Historiae Francorum scriptores,* 5 vols. in fol. (Paris, 1636–1649), I, pp. 172–175, reproduces an earlier German essay, *Hermanni Comitis Nuenarii brevis narratio de origine et sedibus priscorum francorum* (1521). This essay is like a rough sketch for Beatus' discussion of this subject. Paul Joachimsen, in his *Geschichtsauffassung und Geschichtsschreibung in Deutschland unter dem Einfluss des Humanismus* (Leipzig, Berlin,

Beatus reviewed the evidence in the ancient authors, denounced Trithemius' Hunibald as fiction, consulted and quoted Jornandes (Jordanes or Jordanis, the sixth-century author of the *Getica*), Paulus Diaconus, and Liutprand, but rested his demonstration mainly on the evidence of some third-century panegyrics which he himself had published in 1520.[16] These panegyrics constitute even today the most reliable sources for the history of the Franks before their conquest of Gaul.

Beatus was sufficiently awed by the humanist prejudice against quoting documents to deplore the condition of his sources but not enough to exclude them.[17] Committed to the principle of affirming nothing that was not to be found in the testimony of trustworthy authors, he concluded that the Franks were a maritime people who spoke a Germanic language and of whose existence there was no proof before the third century.[18]

This shocking thesis was not immediately welcome in France. Beatus stripped the French of their Trojan ancestry and claimed that Gaul was conquered, settled, and still ruled by a German people. Patriotic French intellectuals resisted this suggestion. Guillaume du Bellay ignored the skepticism of Gaguin, the clear doubts of Emilio, and the scandalous suggestions of Beat-

---

1910), pointed out that in Count Hermann's essay, in the Chronicle of Nauclerus (ca. 1504), in a polemical work of Bebel's (1507), and in the edition of the panegyrics by Cuspinianus in 1513, some of the steps were taken which made Beatus' critical work possible. And it is also true that in these German humanist circles at the turn of the century some fabulous stories of German origins were rejected in favor of the notion "Germani sunt indigeni," after Tacitus. But this point of view was taken for political reasons (*Kulturkampf* against claims of Italian superiority) and not critical historical reasons. As Joachimsen makes clear, Beatus was a pioneer and a loner: he was never understood by his German contemporaries, he belonged to no circle, and had no disciples. To demonstrate that the Franks were a German-speaking people, Beatus quoted some lines of old German in his *Rerum Germanicorum,* this in itself a real novelty: "Otfried's Krist: Nu vvil ich scriban unser heil/ Evangeliono deil/So wir nu hiar bigunnon/In Frenkisga zungon."

[16] Beatus Rhenanus, *Panegyrici veteres* (Basel, Froben, 1520).

[17] "Quae verba depravatissime leguntur in vulgatis exemplaribus." Beatus, *Rerum Germanicorum,* p. 31.

[18] *Ibid.,* p. 29.

us to return to the Trojan story.[19] Jean Bodin, critical of the
Trojan legend but intent upon denying the German origin of
the Franks, explained that they were not foreign conquerors
at all; they were Gauls who had established colonies east of
the Rhine and had later returned to their Celtic homeland.[20]
Guillaume Postel combined the best of both theories: the
Franks were led from burning Troy by Francio, to be sure, but
they were also descended from Gomer, father of the Gauls.
Postel's frantic genealogical efforts to demonstrate his thesis
took him back all the way to Noah. In his account the Franks
are seen crossing the Rhine after centuries of wandering in the
steppes, only to rejoin their blood brothers, the Gauls. Once
again the French nation emerges out of its tumultuous history
one and indivisible.[21]

While such fantasies continued to occupy some of the best
minds of this generation, there were Frenchmen who could accept the fact that very little was known about their ancestors.
Estienne Pasquier in 1560 described the Trojan story as a
"common opinion." He was very skeptical of it, but he thought
the business of arguing about the ancient origins of nations a
waste of time. The Trojan story, he concluded, was probably
mythical and nothing else was certain either. One should really
dismiss the matter entirely and admit one's ignorance.[22]

At this time Pasquier probably had not read Beatus' dissertation, or if he had read it, he came away unconvinced. This is

---

[19] Du Bellay, *Epitomé de l'antiquité des Gaules et de France.*

[20] Bodin, *Methodus*, p. 403. References are to Pierre Mesnard's edition, *Oeuvres philosophiques de Jean Bodin* (Paris, 1951). Caprariis, *Propaganda,* p.
367, attributes the same story of the returning Gauls to Pasquier. Since Caprariis does not support this statement, it is difficult to trace its origin. Clearly
no such view is expressed in the sixteenth-century editions of Pasquier's *Recherches.* Caprariis, however, uses an eighteenth-century edition and it is
just barely possible that the old tale had crept in somewhere.

[21] Guillaume Postel, *L'histoire memorable des expeditions depuis le deluge
faictes par les Gaulois ou Françoys* (Paris, 1552), pp. 52–53. Postel's inspired account owed much to Annius of Viterbo.

[22] Pasquier, *Recherches* (Paris, 1560), pp. 53–55.

quite possible. Beatus presented the sources to his readers, but he lacked the imagination to create history from the scattered references in the panegyrics. One of the obvious difficulties was that the panegyrics, when they first refer to the Franks, describe them as a powerful people. But how could a great tribe suddenly appear out of nowhere, completely unnoticed by all the Roman writers before the third century? Beatus could offer no explanation.[23]

This problem, however, was soon solved. In Paris a group of young jurists-turned-historians expanded Beatus' rudimentary comments into a plausible account of French prehistory. Pasquier soon abandoned his original skepticism; something, after all, could be known about the early Franks. By this time he had obviously studied Beatus. He knew the panegyrics. He could even supply answers to questions which had puzzled Beatus,[24] but his casual remarks were meant only to show that he was aware of the latest work on this subject. For a fuller account one must turn to the work of Pasquier's teacher, Dr. François Hotman.

In 1573 Hotman published his controversial *Franco-Gallia*. In this book the French historian brought Beatus' investigations before a larger audience and solved some of the problems which had puzzled the German philologist.

Using the panegyrics as his main source, Hotman, like Beatus, showed that the Franks had been a seafaring people who had originally inhabited the marshy coast between the Rhine and the Elbe.[25] Hotman controlled the panegyrics with passages in Claudian, Procopius, Flavius Vopiscus, and Sidonius Apollinaris, always careful to indicate his sources and quoting them frequently. Like Beatus, he was struck by the similarity between ancient descriptions of the Chaucii, a tribe known to Pliny, and the panegyrics' descriptions of the Franks. It had

23 Beatus, *Rerum Germanicorum*, p. 29.

24 Pasquier, *Recherches* (Paris, 1569), pp. 30–31.

25 François Hotman, *La Gaule françoise* (Simon Goulart's translation of *Franco-Gallia*) (Cologne, 1574).

occurred to Beatus that the two tribes might somehow be re-
lated.[26] Hotman made sense out of this and other scattered clues
by working on the hypothesis that the Franks must have existed,
judging from their power in the third century, for hundreds of
years. Nothing could be new about them in the third century
except their name. This led him to the conclusion that the most
likely explanation of their sudden appearance was that the
Franks were not a tribe at all, but rather a horde of Germanic
combat-groups, composed, perhaps, of contingents from several
established tribes. These raiders most likely were given the
name of Franks after they had achieved a common notoriety.[27]
This hypothesis still stands today as the most likely explanation.[28]

Dr. Hotman gently ridiculed those naïve souls who still chose
to believe the Trojan legend,[29] and after the publication of his
book it became nearly impossible to repeat the medieval tale in
France. Despite the political connotations of this issue, historians of all parties repudiated the legend. The Catholic Jean
du Tillet, in his posthumous *Mémoires et recherches*, confirmed the findings of the heretic Dr. Hotman.[30] He was especially interested in comparing the customs and institutions of
the Franks with those of other Germanic peoples and, like
Beatus before him, he insisted on the linguistic relationship
between the Franks and the other Germans.[31] As for the word
"Frank" and its sudden appearance, he believes the word to
have come from *Franckhufen*, meaning "free companies." He

[26] Beatus, *Rerum Germanicorum*, p. 35.

[27] Hotman, *La Gaule françoise*, p. 47.

[28] Schmidt, *Geschichte der deutschen Stämme*, p. 433.

[29] "Quant aux autres, qui pour le goust qu'ils ont pris à des fables et contes
faits à plaisir, ont rapporté l'origine des François aux Troyens et à un ne
sais quel Francion fils de Priamus: ie n'en veux dire autre chose, sinon
qu'ils ont plustot fourni de matière à écrire aux Poëtes qu'aux historiens
veritables." Hotman, *La Gaule françoise*, p. 45.

[30] Jean du Tillet, *Les mémoires et recherches* (Rouen, 1578), p. 3.

[31] *Ibid.*, pp. 3–7.

finds the word *Hufen* used in this sense in a Carolingian privilege accorded to the city of Paris.[32]

The royal historiographer and physician Nicolas Vignier was a Protestant who abjured his faith in order, it would seem, to return to France and exercise his profession. Vignier was probably the most painstaking and critical historian of his generation. At work for some twenty-five years on his immense *Bibliothèque historiale* (1588), he published several books on French medieval history before the appearance of his *chef d'oeuvre*. His *Sommaire de l'histoire des françois* begins with a sixteen-page essay on the origin, condition, and habitat of the ancient French. Vignier has little patience with those who invent fables and he denounces them roundly.[33] He knows the work of his predecessors, quotes copiously from the panegyrics and other sources, and, on the whole, follows Hotman's interpretations. He can add very little to the existing information. His contribution lies in his special concern with historical method. He is always careful to establish the degree of probability of any assertion about the past. His fear of committing an error borders on hypercriticism. Thus, when he is forced to come to some conclusions after reviewing the historiography of the problem, he hesitates. He is not sure that the matter has been proved beyond doubt. Hotman's and Du Tillet's explanations of the word "Frank" seem to him probable rather than certain, founded as they are on conjecture. Finally, "à fin de ne sortir hors de ce propos sans aucune resolution," and after another four hundred words of caution and qualification, he concludes that "il semble que nous pouvons avec quelque raison tirer en

---

[32] *Ibid.*, p. 6.

[33] "Quant aux longues & prolixes narrations que certains escrivains Allemans & Flemants de ce siecle ont digerees des fables de Trittemius & d'Annius de Viterbe, ou d'autres aucteurs . . . pour extraire les François de Troyens . . .: ie les quite a ceux qui font estat & gain de mettre toute matiere en oeuvre, sans discerner la vraye d'avec la faulse. . . ." Vignier, *Sommaire*. The pages of the prefatory essay are not numbered.

consequence bien apparente, que le pays originel des François estoit en la Germanie."[34]

By 1579 the rejection of the Trojan legend had become a standard feature in the learned books of Protestant, Catholic, Gallican, royalist, and *politique* scholars. Moreover, by this time even writers of popular histories designed for the entertainment of a large reading public found it necessary to reject the legend. One of the most popular of these writers, François de Belleforest, begins his *Annales* (1579) with the announcement that he has made up his mind "to say nothing without very convincing proof and without the guarantee of authentic and illustrious authorities." The French right now, he observes, are interested only in serious matters. To prove to his detractors that he "has looked into more books than they think," Belleforest begins his book with "Divers Considerations on the Origins of the French" in which he emphatically rejects the Trojan legend on the most scholarly grounds.[35] Clearly the entire question was settled by 1579. The royal historiographer Vignier was not ordered to concoct a more glorious or less Germanic ancestry for the French nation. Under Henri IV, Vignier retained his position until his death in 1596. His suc-

---

[34] *Loc. cit.*

[35] ". . . suis resolu de ne rien proposer sans raison fort evidente, & sans avoir garant & autheur autentique & illustre, puisqu'il faut escrire aux François, hommes de grand esprit & lesquels ne se payent à present que de choses hautes & serieuses; toutefois pour le passetemps des curieux [scholars], & afin que les envieux [those who do not think him learned enough] cognoissent que i'ay plus fueilleté de livres qu'ils ne pensent, & ay fait, suyvant ma coustume, de grandes recherches. . . ." François de Belleforest, *Les grandes annales et histoire generale de France*, 2 vols. (Paris, 1579), I, f. lv. Belleforest, who obviously knows how to please and flatter his readers, not only tells them how high-minded and serious they are but must find a way of making them swallow the bitter pill of his debunking; he does this by reminding his readers of their French virility which ought not to stand for "delicate courtly fables" of foreign origin: "Et entre nous, qui portons le titre masle de France, haults à main, & belliqueux, encore s'est venuë loger ceste delicate courtisane fable. . . ."

cessor in the office of royal historiographer, Jean de Serres, also rejected the legend.[36]

The achievement of the sixteenth-century historians went far beyond the rejection of a particular legend. What they had established, in this case as in many others, was the authority of historical criticism. Against this authority there was no appeal: kings and popular writers alike acknowledged this. In the seventeenth century, however, in the reigns of Louis XIII and Louis XIV, the authority of historical criticism was questioned and even rebelled against. The Trojan story could once again be affirmed or denied at will by the most reputable historians. The painstaking researches of the earlier scholars were often disregarded. At best, historians would offer their readers a choice among a number of theories, including the most preposterous fabrications.[37]

François de Mézeray (1610–1683), perhaps the most highly regarded French historian of the seventeenth century, adopted a position full of ambiguity; he assured his readers that he knew the Trojan story to be full of fables, but he was persuaded that old legends must be, however distantly, founded in fact.[38] He was unable to choose between the romantic stories of the chroniclers and the critical accounts of the sixteenth-century historians. It is difficult to say to what extent Mézeray was familiar with the work of Vignier, Hotman, and others, since he did not acknowledge his sources. Much of the time when he was dealing with medieval history, he merely paraphrased a French translation of Paolo Emilio's *De rebus gestis*. In this case, how-

[36] De Serres, *Inventaire général* (Paris, 1597).

[37] By 1676 there were twelve such theories, according to Nathan Edelman in *Attitudes of Seventeenth-Century France toward the Middle Ages* (New York, 1946), p. 77. He concludes that the Trojan legend persisted in historical writing throughout the seventeenth century.

[38] ". . . je sais que ce narré est plein de fables et d'anachronismes: mais je suis persuadé qu'il n'y a gueres de vieux contes qui n'ayant quelque fondement dans la verité. . . ." Mézeray, *Histoire de France* (Amsterdam, 1692), p. 194.

ever, he rejected Emilio's etymological explanation (Cicero's Frangones). As for the Germanic theory, it seemed like a good possibility to him. He left it up to his readers to come to a conclusion, perhaps because he wished to offend no one.[39]

Other seventeenth-century historians found it easier to make up their minds. The Jesuit Taraut, in his *Annales de France*, sought to combine the findings of the sixteenth-century scholars with the new patriotic needs of the French court. In his book, which is dedicated to Louis XIII, Taraut handles the question of French origins very cautiously. First he gives a summary of the work of Beatus, Hotman, and Vignier, without acknowledging his debt to these heretic scholars. Then he denies that the Franks were ever a Germanic people through the familiar device of the returning Gauls. "Although I say that the Franks came from Westphalia, Frisia, and Saxony," writes this clever opportunist, "I do not hold that they had always lived there; but maintain that the Franks had been a colony established by the Gauls."[40]

A less subtle approach is demonstrated in Jacques de Charron's *Histoire universelle*. Here the Trojan story is told with gusto and earnest conviction by a writer who claims to have read Vignier, Hotman, Belleforest, and Du Tillet. His thesis is simply that all the medieval authorities who were discredited during the last century should now be reinstated.[41]

Under official patronage, the writing of history during the *grand siècle* was often divorced from the practice of historical criticism, especially when the subject was of interest to the state. This explains why Fréret's paper at the Academy of Inscriptions was held to be subversive in 1714. Fréret's account of Frankish prehistory was similar to those of Vignier and Hot-

---

[39] *Ibid.*, p. 196.

[40] See note 6 above.

[41] Jacques de Charron, *Histoire universelle* (Paris, 1621), pp. 194ff.

man.[42] The main difference was Fréret's complete reluctance to refer to his sources. He used the panegyrics, even quoted them occasionally, but he did not say where the reader could find them. The same is true of his attitude toward secondary sources. He allowed that Vignier had given him "many ideas," but he did not credit Vignier or anyone else with any part of his account.[43] It is fairly clear from the tone of his paper that the denial of Trojan origins in private was not a revolutionary thesis in his day.[44] Fréret wanted to prove that it was possible to come to some fairly definite conclusions in this matter. Discouraged by his jail sentence, he was said to have prudently avoided such touchy subjects for the rest of his life.[45]

Clearly, the development of French historiography since 1500 does not show a pattern of simple progress. The question of national origins may be thought an exception, but this is not so. In the composition of general histories, the same high critical standards are displayed in the books of the earlier historians and the same relapse into fiction can be found in the seventeenth-century works.[46] This is not to say that the Trojan Franks were not a political issue; they were. But so was all history, as Bishop Bossuet made perfectly clear. While the

---

[42] Nicolas Fréret, *Oeuvres complètes*, ed. M. de Septchênes (Paris, 1796), V, pp. 155ff.

[43] References to Vignier in Fréret, *Oeuvres*, pp. 163, 293.

[44] *Ibid.*, p. 155.

[45] See the preface by Bougainville, *ibid.*, I, p. A4.

[46] Mézeray, for example, resurrects the giants of the medieval chroniclers. He retells the story of Roland killing the giant Ferragut and finds nothing in this fabulous tale "qu'on puisse absolument convaincre de faux." *Histoire de France* (Paris, 1643), I, p. 174. The medieval source of this story had been subjected to expert historical criticism by Papire Masson in 1577. Masson demonstrated that the chronicle was a forgery in *Annalium libri quattuor* (Paris, 1577), pp. 97–101, cited in Ronzy, *Masson*. Nicolas Vignier's account of the engagement at Roncevaux and of Court Roland's actions in *Sommaire* was a bare paragraph, stripped of all legendary material, in which he followed Eginhard.

standards of historical writing declined, the memory of the old historians became extinct. The gradual subordination of culture to the demands of the monarchy in the century which extended from the promulgation of the Edict of Nantes to its revocation successfully obscured the achievements of Renaissance culture in France.

An easy method
for the understanding
of all history

Fifth chapter

Ⅰt seems fairly clear that the advocates of the New History made a large place for erudition in the "perfect history" they desired. The old histories in their view bore more resemblance to fiction than to fact. There was no room for fiction in the new histories. The truth—laboriously arrived at through scholarly cooperation—was indispensable. But the purely antiquarian pursuit of facts was not their goal. Erudition was the necessary first step, but no more than that, in the new method which was to allow its practitioners to explain, eventually, all of past human experience: history was not merely research, but, ultimately, "the soul of human actions."[1]

The old histories were worthless not only because they were not founded on research but also because they failed to explain the "causes and motives" of events. That was the difference between mere *chroniqueurs* and true *historiographes*. A *chroniqueur* could be truthful enough and punctilious in his research, but to become a true historian he had to do more. To establish and set down one observed fact after another was one kind of achievement. To go beyond this and to explain how one event led to another—to explain causes in history—was a task of a different order, and the only one really worthy of the true historian.

The issue here is the understanding of universal history in the sixteenth century. From the point of view of Vignier or La Popelinière, there was no precedent in the ancient or medieval writers for the sort of general history they envisaged. A few among the Ancients had written of the desirability of general history (Polybius) or even claimed to be writing universal history. Diodorus of Sicily "boasted of writing a universal history," comments Vignier, "but all he did in fact was to give a verbose and partisan account of his Greeks and Sicilians," hardly touching upon "the affairs of the Romans and other nations."[2]

It is true that the scope of the classical histories was not global. It is also true that the ancient Greek historians did not reach very far back into the past.[3] But, above all else, in the sixteenth

---

[1] La Popelinière, *Histoire des histoires*, p. 53, and *Histoire de France* (Arras?, 1582), p. 4. He makes it clear that "les causes des accidens humains s'entretiennent d'un lien eternel et connu de peu de gens"; it is this lien, this bond or connection between the particular events of human history, which must be sought out by those who wish to approach the "modelle d'un vray historiographe."

[2] Vignier is citing Juan Luis Vives here, in the preface to the first volume of the *Bibliothèque historiale* (Paris, 1588).

[3] Collingwood noted that the method of the Greek historians "tied them on a tether whose length was the length of living memory." *Idea of History*, p. 26. M. I. Finley comments on the Greek interest in the distant past:

century an educated man could view human history—was
forced to view it—from a perspective which was drastically
different from that of the ancient writers. The Greek wars which
appeared so momentous to Thucydides and even the rise of
Roman power which Polybius thought of as the only event of
universal significance in human experience, these events had
already been upstaged long ago in the new scenarios of world
history written by Christian bishops like Eusebius of Caesarea,
in which Gentiles and pagans appeared only as adjuncts of the
history of the people of God.[4]

Humanist educators had tried to revive the perspectives of
the ancient historians, but no amount of absorption in the pagan
classics could erase the reality of Jewish and Christian history.
Was the plague which struck the Athenians an event of truly
universal significance? The Hebrew historians knew nothing of
it. Conversely, the Greek historians knew nothing of the plague
which struck the Egyptians. How could the pagan histories lay
claim to universality when they ignored the momentous events
of Hebrew and Christian history? How, on the other hand,
could the sacred histories be regarded as universal when they
ignored the civilizations of Greece and Rome? The early Christian writers had already faced this difficulty, but now, a thousand years later, the difficulty was increased no end by the
addition of so much more historical material. The educated
Frenchman could not conceal the fact that the thousand-year-
long history of the French was more important to him than the

---

". . . it would be a great mistake to explain our superior knowledge of
Mycenae by reference to scientific advances. Technically, Schliemann and
Sir Arthur Evans had little at their disposal which was not available to fifth
century Athenians." "Myth, Memory and History," *History and Theory* 4
(1965), p. 292. Momigliano extends a similar judgment to all ancient
historiography: "It seems to me," he says in connection with Thucydides,
"that this approach to history, as basically contemporary history, is the type
that prevailed throughout antiquity." *Histoire et historiens*, p. 27.

[4] Thus the Age of Pericles enters Eusebius' vision only in the form of the
notation, "Pericles moritur," in *Hieronymi chronicon*, ed. R. Helm (Berlin,
1956), p. 115.

history of the Greeks and Romans; and, if the truth were known, to his mind even the history of the Jews paled in significance beside that of the French.

The histories of the European nations and cities had to be considered, all of them, as part of universal history; and to this third large body of historical facts one had to add, in good conscience, the histories of the Arabs and the Turks who played perhaps as large a role in the history of Mediterranean Europe as had the Romans or the Greeks. Beyond the Arabs and Turks, waiting in the wings but impossible to ignore, there were the histories of obscure but powerful neighbors to be written—Tartars, Huns, Russians—and the histories of the newly discovered African, American, and Far Eastern nations as well. Clearly, if one wanted to tell the whole story of mankind, a new perspective would have to be devised from which to order this mass of recalcitrant historical subjects.

Could one do this without impiety? Were there not, after all, some generally accepted, and divinely revealed, views on the meaning of human history? Yes, of course. Nonetheless, this philosophy of history, which bore the forceful imprint of the mind of the bishop of Hippo, had never really exerted much influence in the domain of secular history. As Momigliano has written, "the traditional forms of higher historiography did not attract the Christians. They invented new ones." The Christian interpretation of history remained confined, on the whole, to a specific kind of historical narrative: ecclesiastical history. The bishops did not try to Christianize ordinary political history.[5] Outside of the field of church history, the medieval historian retained the Graeco-Roman conception of history as a contemporary record of events,[6] and there is hardly an example,

[5] A. D. Momigliano, "Pagan and Christian Historiography in the Fourth Century A.D.," in *The Conflict between Paganism and Christianity*, ed. A. D. Momigliano (Oxford, 1963), p. 88.

[6] *Ibid.*, p. 89. Momigliano points out that in the sixth century Procopius writes military and political history from a basically pagan outlook and that the humanists in the fifteenth and sixteenth centuries, when they re-

before the twelfth century, of an historian trying to interpret the events of secular history according to the theology of Augustine.[7] Even Otto of Freising, who does make such an attempt in his *Chronica*, cannot quite be said to have succeeded; and he will have no successors.[8]

In a very suggestive recent study, the argument has been put forward that the medieval clerical chronicler "had no system into which particular explanations might be fitted" and that he was not concerned about causal processes because he "didn't know they existed."[9] "Action in the clerical view," writes William J. Brandt, "did not originate in the precedent situation; it acted as a disturbance to that situation, originating, in some peculiar way, outside it. The peculiar shape that entries take in the universalizing chronicles" cannot be explained away as "a superficial" or "a fortuitous characteristic. It is not a product of the impossible task of dealing with an unlimited subject matter. The proof of this fact," in Brandt's view, "is that the clerical chronicler broke up his materials in a very similar way when he was not writing a universalizing chronicle—when he was presenting the elements of what a modern historian would regard as a single line of action."[10]

---

discovered the pagan historians, "rediscovered something for which there was no plain Christian alternative." Thus, "the conditions which made Machiavelli and Guicciardini possible originated in the fourth century A.D." Johannes Spörl makes the point that "Geschichte im engeren Sinne ist also auch im Mittelalter der 'Augenzeugenbericht'." *Grundformen hochmittelalterlicher Geschichtsanschauung* (Munich, 1935), p. 18.

[7] Spörl, *Grundformen*, p. 39; see also A. D. van den Brincken, *Studien zur lateinischen Weltchronistik* (Düsseldorf, 1957), p. 223.

[8] Otto "denkt universal, ohne zu merken, dass er universal im deutschen Sinne denkt." Spörl, *Grundformen*, p. 45. "Nach dem 12. Jahrhundert hat es im Abendland keine wissenschaftliche Chronographie mehr gegeben, man suchte weder die Geschichte zu deuten, noch bemühte man sich um ihre Chronologie. Das Schulwesen übte den allein beherrschenden Einfluss auf die Gestaltung der Universalgeschichtsschreibung aus." Van den Brincken, *Studien*, p. 230.

[9] William J. Brandt, *The Shape of Medieval History* (New Haven, Conn., 1966), p. 51.

[10] *Ibid.*, pp. 73, 76.

This, I think, is very persuasive. Certainly the failure of the medieval chroniclers to perceive the world as process drew the scorn of the New Historians who demanded an *historia integra* to replace the chaos of existing historical narratives.[11] This is the problem tackled by Jean Bodin in his *Method for the Easy Comprehension of History* in 1566.[12] At the outset of this work, the author discards the theological interpretations of human history. Such interpretations are not valid, in his view, because history—human history, that is—is a discipline which has nothing in common with the study of God or of nature. Human history "explains the actions of man as he lives in society" (*actiones hominis in societate vitam agentis explicat*); natural history on the other hand, studies a subject of a totally different sort, namely, "causes hidden in nature"; while the subject of divine history is something else entirely. These three disciplines each lead to a different kind of result. The truths which may be

---

[11] On this demand for a new, universal, integral history before Bodin see Kelley, "Historia Integra."

[12] Bodin, *Methodus*. References are to the critical edition given by Mesnard, *Oeuvres philosophiques de Jean Bodin*. An English translation of the *Methodus* was made by the late Beatrice Reynolds, *Method for the Easy Comprehension of History* (New York, 1945). For a survey of modern scholarship on Bodin's historical theory, one should consult not only Mesnard's introduction, but also Brown's study, *The "Methodus . . ." of Jean Bodin*, which is the only monograph specifically devoted to the *Methodus*. Among other important studies of Bodin's thought which deal in one way or another with the *Methodus*, there are Aldo Garosci, *J. Bodin* (Milan, 1934); Moreau-Reibel, *J. Bodin*; and M. E. Kamp, *Die Staatswirtschaftslehre J. Bodins* (Bonn, 1949). Adalbert Klempt's important book, *Die Säkularisierung der universalhistorischen Auffassung* (Göttingen, 1960), goes further than any other study in placing Bodin's *Methodus* into the general context of evolving theories about the nature of universal history in the sixteenth century. The most recent study is Franklin, *Bodin and the Sixteenth Century Revolution*, which ought to be read together with my review article in *Studi francesi* 8 (1964), pp. 302–307. There is no point in reviewing the scant facts known to us about Bodin's life; these can be found in the works cited above. One need remember only that Bodin's father was a master tailor in Angers; that Bodin studied in Paris as a young man and then studied law and taught it at Toulouse; and finally that he arrived in Paris and became an *avocat* at the *parlement* shortly before the composition of the *Methodus,* in his early thirties. He was, then, a bourgeois, a child prodigy, a humanist, a jurist, and a newly received member of the *robin* establishment.

reached in the field of human history are probable truths only; natural history produces logically necessary results; the conclusions of divine history belong to the realm of faith.[13]

Bodin leaves natural history to the scientists and divine history to the theologians.[14] Thus the history of man in society stands alone, stripped of any theological significance.[15] This history "is mostly the result of the will of men," which "is never the same" and escapes prediction. "For every day new laws are created, new customs, new institutions, new rites."[16] If only this immense variety of human actions could be reduced to some order!

The difficulty lay, in the first place, in the data transmitted by the historians; they were fragmentary, faulty, and contradictory. If only it were possible to control the historians' information with data of a more trustworthy sort.[17] Bodin explores the possibilities of geography, anthropology, biology, and even astrology in the hope of reducing historical change to some general laws. Could one account for the different histories of the Egyptians, Romans, and Germans by analysing the geographical environment in which these peoples functioned—or their racial characteristics, or their physical constitution, or even the conjunction of the stars?

The temptation is very great. Occasionally Bodin cannot refrain from sketching out some grand hypothesis. The past six

[13] Bodin, *Methodus*, p. 114.

[14] *Ibid.*, p. 115.

[15] For a discussion of the importance of theology in German Protestant university teaching of history before the publication of Bodin's treatise, see Klempt, who also emphasizes the revolutionary part played by the *Methodus*: "Durch seine methodische Beschränkung auf die rein profanhistorische Betrachtungsweise bei der Erforschung der Menschheitsgeschichte kommt Bodin . . . zum ausdrücklichen Verzicht auf jede theologische Deutung des universalhistorischen Zusammenhangs. . . ." *Säkularisierung*, p. 43.

[16] ". . . at humana historia quod magna sui parte fluit ab hominum voluntate, quae semper sui dissimilis est, nullum exitum habet: sed quotidie novae leges, novi mores, nova instituta, novi ritus oboriuntur." Bodin, *Methodus*, p. 115.

[17] *Ibid.*, p. 140.

thousand years of human history, he speculates, seem to fall naturally into three main periods of about two thousand years each. (He remains indecisive on the question of the world's age, contenting himself in the end with citing the various conflicting estimates.) In the first of these epochs civilization flourished in the southern regions (Mesopotamia, Egypt) and its distinguishing mark was the preponderance of religion and of wisdom; but this was also the age when man's conquest of nature took its first large strides, especially in the realm of astronomy. In the course of the second epoch, the center of gravity of world civilization shifted across the Mediterranean. Its specific features were the foundation of city-states, the making of laws, and colonial expansion. Finally, in the epoch whose beginning coincided roughly with the beginning of the Christian era, civilization shifted still further north, to other races, and it was distinguished by the evolution of warfare and technology. Whether this pattern of events was determined in some way or not, Bodin cannot tell. But the fact is there, easily observed, even if the causes are obscure, he concludes.[18]

Such generalizations are rare in the *Method*. Typically, the author will lead up to something of this sort in twenty pages of tightly argued text bristling with quotations from ancient sources which he controls, and often rejects, by confrontation with modern authorities. Then, having assembled a vast amount of information, much of it pointing toward a deterministic conclusion, he stops short, utters doubts, hedges with qualifications, briefly explains his hypothesis—but ends up calling for more research to resolve the issue.[19] After one discussion of this sort, on the relationship between the movement of the stars and human affairs, he concludes regretfully: "There is no end to such researches. There is some relationship no doubt between the great [astral] conjunctions and the chief military and political

[18] *Ibid.*, pp. 154–155.

[19] *Ibid.*, p. 140. Here Bodin explores the relationship between geography and history.

events; but there is no way of discovering . . . which region is
singled out for specific [astral] influences: therefore it is quite
impossible to get any solid data by following the principles of
the astrologers. On the other hand," he adds, "I have no doubt
that a better method could be worked out someday as a result
of a great deal of additional information."[20] He concludes on
an optimistic note: "It should be sufficient to collect all the data
we have concerning memorable events and to compare these
with the great conjunctions of the stars . . . to create a more
perfected science of the nature and character of peoples."[21]

The notion that climate may determine history is attractive
to Bodin, but he never succumbs to it. Although he compiles a
great deal of information around this hypothesis, he never
comes to a conclusion. He always holds himself in check by
referring to the complexity of human motives, to man's ability
to overcome almost any challenge created by his environment.[22]
Considering how cautious he is toward his own generalizations,
it comes as no surprise to find Bodin attacking the lame con-
structions of his predecessors.

Among the older schemes for the narration of world history,
the most widely used was that of the four kingdoms or empires.
The destiny of mankind, according to this theory, was tied to a
succession of four world-empires. Babylon, Persia, Greece, and
Rome were usually designated as the empires in question. The
advantage of this scheme was that it satisfied, in principle at
least, the Christian need for a universal scope of narration and
at the same time, made it unnecessary to do any actual thinking
about the innumerable states which cropped up in the chroni-

---

[20] *Ibid.,* p. 166. Elsewhere Bodin rejects astrology explicitly: ". . . postremo
Ptolemaei ac veterum errores confutabimus, qui mores populorum ad
Zodiaci partes, quas cuique regioni tribuunt, referri putant opportere." *Ibid.,*
p. 140.

[21] *Ibid.,* p. 167.

[22] Compare Klempt, *Säkularisierung,* p. 43, Moreau-Reibel, *J. Bodin,* p. 73,
and Kamp, *Staatswirtschaftslehre J. Bodins,* p. 38, who also observes that
Bodin avoids the trap of a simple geographical determinism.

cles. One had it on the best of authorities (Daniel 2:36–40)
that God's plan allowed for only four empires to succeed each
other in this world. For a twelfth-century German bishop this
theory had an obvious appeal: since the Roman empire was
prophetically certified to be the last on earth, it must still exist;
and what worthier candidate for this role could one imagine
than the German empire itself? The same appeal still exercised
its attraction in Bodin's time among German theologians and
historians.[23]

"To affirm, with Melanchthon, that the Germans have the
most powerful monarchy in the world is absurd, and it is even
more absurd to pretend that this is the Roman empire," writes
Bodin, supporting his statement with a crushing weight of evidence. To tease the Germans he makes a plausible case for calling the Turks rather than the Germans the inheritors of Rome:
"Whether we define monarchy by the power of its arms, the size
of its resources, the fertility of its territory, the list of its victories, the number of its inhabitants or, following only the
etymology of the word, by the fact that it applies to Daniel's
fatherland or to the empire of Babylon, or using the sole criterion of the most widespread authority, one has to admit that
Daniel's prophecy can be applied more accurately to the Grand
Turk." In any case, Bodin points out, there have been more
than four empires, some of them greater than Babylon. What
about the Arabs, whose empire extended over almost all Africa
and a large part of Asia? And why should one leave out the
Tartars? Because they were far from Babylon? But the Germans
were even farther.[24]

The refutation of the four monarchies theory serves only as
a curtain raiser; far more important is Bodin's attack against

---

[23] See E. Menke-Glückert, *Die Geschichtsschreibung der Reformation und
Gegenreformation* (Leipzig, 1912), and Klempt, *Säkularisierung*. One of the
most influential of the German world chronicles was the *Chronicon* composed
by Johannes Carion (Wittenberg, 1532), which was edited by Melanchthon
and of which Bodin cites a 1540 edition.

[24] Bodin, *Methodus*, pp. 224–225.

the myth of the Golden Age. This very old myth, adapted to Christian theology—once again through the intermediary of Daniel's vision of a statue with a golden head, a silver chest, bronze thighs, iron legs, and feet of clay—served as a symbolic summary of the Christian philosophy of history, according to which mankind degenerated through a succession of stages from the purity of the Golden Age (or the innocence of Paradise) to the last age, always identified with the present, an age of immorality and general corruption whose end was soon to come.

Such a myth corresponded, no doubt, to certain psychological and historical realities during the Middle Ages. This was less true in the sixteenth century, especially in the world of the humanist intellectuals, imbued as it was with a vision of a new Golden Age, a renovation and restoration of letters and piety coming after a long period of darkness. Bodin's emotional commitment to the present and to the future, his affirmation of the new enlightenment, is remarkable only because it is so unequivocally stated. Otherwise it is already a cliché. His attack against the theory of historical decadence is not carried out on the ground of conviction or rhetoric: he argues from history.

He begins with the bald statement that "the so-called Golden Age, in comparison with the present, may well appear to be an Iron Age." The testimony of the Old Testament and of the ancient poets concerning this early period is hardly favorable; the behavior of figures like Cham and Nimrod, Jupiter and Hercules, is nothing but savagery. "And lest one think that our opinion is founded only on fables, let us consult Thucydides . . ." Bodin offers. In Thucydides he finds specific evidence to show that the Greeks had been savages. Piracy and brigandage were respected professions and right lay solely in a man's ability to defend himself, weapons in hand. "There you have your famous centuries of Gold and Silver! Men lived dispersed in the fields and forests like wild beasts, and had no private property except that which they could hang on to by force and crime: it has taken a long time to pull them away from this savage and barbarous way of life and to accustom them to civilized behavior and to a well-regulated society such as we now have everywhere."

Clearly, if the course of history were to be understood as a constant degeneration, contemporary morality, customs, and laws should be worse, not better, than those of the earliest times. This is demonstrably not the case. One need only consult the annals and documents of the Ancients to find the worst excesses practiced, including human sacrifice and vicious circus games.

Not only the virtue but also the knowledge of his contemporaries, Bodin contends, is equal to that of the Ancients. In his time culture has reached such brilliance, after centuries of somnolence, that there never was anything like it. Ironically, he confides in an aside, even the Goths (in this case he means the Scandinavians), who were once responsible for the death of culture, now seek humanists everywhere. The Ancients made admirable discoveries in their time, but modern discoveries equal theirs and even surpass them. Among these, he cites the mariner's compass, the discovery of new worlds, the expansion of trade, artillery (compared to which the machines of the ancients are toys), and the techniques for working metals and cloth. The invention of printing alone is worth all the inventions of the Ancients. It is an error to think that mankind is degenerating.[25]

For Bodin, it would seem that if there is any pattern in human history, it is a pattern of progress, but he does not know enough to be sure of this. He also considers the possibility of a cyclical pattern of alternating growth and decline. In the end he opts for neither and leaves the issue unresolved.[26] The movement of history is a subject which he brings up only in short polemic bursts when he is attacking some unexamined notion. In this respect his work is negative. He wipes the slate clean of speculations. The theological or mythical interpretations of his-

---

[25] *Ibid.,* pp. 226–228.

[26] Compare Klempt, *Säkularisierung,* p. 69.

tory, already rejected in practice by several generations of humanists who simply ignored universal history as a genre, are now taken to task in a frontal attack to make way for new interpretations which are to be founded on historical research.

Bodin rejects the traditional motives for the study of history. The calculation of the world's end,[27] the illustration of God's plan, the erection of memorials to the glory of princes and saints, all these cease to be important objectives for historical research. His purpose is to explain the rise and fall of states and the growth and decline of civilization[28] and to explain these in a purely secular manner, without reference to divine providence or Fortuna. The mind of God remains an impenetrable mystery and "nothing is due to chance."[29]

Universal history is no longer universal in the sense of being chronologically complete; it is now universal because it takes into account all known societies, past and present. In Bodin's definition, universal history is not a hallowed preserve, a special treatment of the past. It is simply general history. The phrase has no special technical connotation; general history is different from particular history only in the scope of its subject, and even that is fairly loosely defined as either "the comparison of several peoples with each other, such as the Persians, the Greeks and the Egyptians" or, more broadly, the study of all peoples whose actions have come down to us.[30]

The Hebrew prophets and the Christian bishops were able to embrace millenia in their historical vision only at the cost of selecting very narrowly the kind of thing they wrote about: the saintliness of God's people, the wickedness of others. How could Bodin make sense of the mass of data he was preparing

[27] Such calculations are both stupid and impious in his opinion: ". . . sed haec subtiliùs inquirere . . . non minùs ineptum quià impium videtur." *Ibid.*, p. 241.

[28] *Ibid.*, p. 227.

[29] ". . . quanquam nihil fortuitem esse potest. . . ." *Ibid.*, p. 123.

[30] *Ibid.*, p. 115. In the same spirit, Belleforest speaks of writing the *histoire universelle de la France*, in *Annales*, p. 1091B.

to assault without some form of selectivity? The chaos of human history had bewildered the medieval chroniclers. How much more confusing should it seem to Bodin, whose curiosity extended to so many more empires, republics, and tribes, who added new continents and religions to the medieval store of historical knowledge, and who thought so much more worth recording.

There is no doubt that Bodin's method creates enormous difficulties. Most of these have never been overcome. Still, he is not entirely helpless; he does, after all, employ a principle of selection. Only partly conscious and not without roots in ancient and medieval culture, this principle lies in his use of the concept of civilization.

Where does universal history begin? Bodin's answer is less equivocal than that of the bishops who could never quite make up their minds whether to begin with the Creation, Adam's expulsion, or Abraham's emergence. Unencumbered by the genealogical calculations which had been so important to both Christian and pagan antiquarians, Bodin can cut through myth and eschatology by posing the question in an entirely secular way. Universal history is not a machine, manipulated by inevitable forces as it had been all along and as it was to be again in the nineteenth century.[31]

He asks merely: where should our study of the human past begin? And he answers: it should begin where there is the first evidence of civilization. First, "as the beginnings of politics, of the sciences and of the arts—of civilization [*humanitas*], in short—seem to lie with the Chaldeans, the Assyrians, the Phoenicians and the Egyptians, we shall study their ancient history. . . ." The student should then go on to study "the history of the Hebrew people, but in such a way as to grasp the principles of their political organization rather than those of their religion." After the Hebrews come the Medes, Persians, Hindus, and Scythians, then the Greeks, Italians, Celts, Germans,

---

[31] See the interesting suggestion of M. P. Gilmore in "Freedom and Determinism in Renaissance Historians," *Studies in the Renaissance* 3 (1956).

Arabs, Turks, Tartars, and Muscovites, and finally the Americans, the Africans (below the Sahara), and the populations of the Indies.[32]

Here for the first time is a proposal for the study of universal history which embraces the past of all mankind. The proposal is a practical one; working only with such information as has survived the ravages of time (he knows very well that these remaining records are only a small fragment), Bodin asks only those questions which can be answered by the historian. He wishes to establish how states rise and fall, how culture and technology prosper or decline. Then, without regard for prophecies or philosophical doctrines, one should try to see what factors were responsible for success or failure in each case. Eventually, the results of such studies, however fragmentary, could provide valuable precepts for contemporary life. For Bodin, human history does have a meaning. It is the story, tortuous at times, of the slow growth of that fragile treasure, civilization.

Bodin's theory of civilization can be summed up as follows: the first impulse toward civilization, the first motive for change in human society—the leaven of human history—is to be located in man's instincts and first of all in the instinct of self-preservation. Pushed by instinct, man first wants to provide for his necessities. Then he goes on to desire some superfluous things, without which life would be too harsh. Then he looks for comfort and, finally, he wants luxury. Thus grows the desire to acquire riches. Pushed by acquisitiveness, mankind creates civilization. At a first, rudimentary level, men protect themselves from illness and want. Hunting, cattle raising, farming, building techniques, athletics, and medicine are invented. At a second stage, commerce, industry, and technology are developed. Finally, civilization reaches its climax: culture and other luxuries are created.[33] To satisfy these growing needs, men

---

[32] Bodin, *Methodus*, p. 117.

[33] "Primi generis actiones ad eas artes referentur quae ad tuendam hominum

must organize themselves into ever more complex societies and all their actions tend toward defending this society which is the source of all their satisfactions, from the primitive satisfaction of eating to the refined satisfaction of music making.[34]

Bodin is unquestionably a partisan of civilization. Peace, private property, culture—these are his values. His book contains in embryonic form most of the precepts of later liberalisms. This is not to say that he thinks like Voltaire or Jeremy Bentham. Scholastic philosophy, the science of numbers, and Jewish mysticism compound the obscurities and contradictions which abound in his treatise. The ideas which form the core of Bodin's historical philosophy have not yet hardened into dogma. Unlike Voltaire, he is not willing to reduce the great ages of humanity to the number of four. And, while he considers progress a fact, he has a much keener feeling for its fragility than will many of his modern successors. Is there not a great danger inherent in the progress of civilization itself? Does not civilization make men soft and vulnerable to the attacks of more barbarous nations? Bodin hesitates to come to conclusions and leaves all issues open, pending further research.

---

vitam, morbosque & offensiones depelendas pertinent: ut venatio, pecuaria, agricultura, aedificatio, gymnastica, medicina. Secundum genus ad institoriam, gubernatoriam, lanificia & fabriles artes. Tertium ad cultum & victum splendidiorem atque omnino ad quaestuarias artes, quibus opes parare & partis magnificè uti docenur: in quo superiorum artium perfectio versatur." *Ibid.*, p. 120.

[34] *Ibid.*, pp. 120–121.

A comparative history of civilizations

Sixth chapter

$\mathbf{B}$odin's *Method* was, to the best of my knowledge, the first book published to advance a theory of universal history based on a purely secular study of the growth of civilization. Such a view of history was by no means uncommon among the humanists and jurists who dominated the intellectual world of Paris in Bodin's time. Still, Bodin published his book first. He also expounded the new theory more systematically than anyone else—so much so that some of his contemporaries were inclined to reproach him for being too systematic, too much the *'docteur contemplatif*, as La Popelinière put it. Whatever its short-comings, the *Method* was always read and respected by people who thought about history in the sixteenth century. Precisely because his attempts at generalization were so ambitious, Bodin invited confirmation and refutation on the part of working historians. He was the Max Weber of his time.

Among the books published, as it were, in the wake of Bodin's *Method*, Loys Le Roy's *Vicissitude* is the one in which the concept of civilization is developed most fully. In this book, written in French, the word *civilité* is employed in the title it-self, which describes the scope of the book: it is a universal history of "change from the time when civilization began to the present."[1]

In 1575, then, nine years after the first publication of Bodin's *Method*, it was no longer necessary to rehearse the ponderous arguments about the nature of universal history. One could already take for granted those points Bodin so laboriously demonstrated: that history was a secular discipline, that it did not deal with Creation and Apocalypse or with the fulfillment of Daniel's prophecy; that it was not to be merely a compilation of the ancient annalists; and that its chief objective was the study of society in its broadest sense.

Le Roy's book does just that, and yet it is certainly not a good book. There are few new facts here and the author does not have much critical sense. The book is not, like the *Method*, an example of the most daring thinking of the time. However, what Le Roy lacks in sharpness and common sense, he makes up for in enthusiasm. This respectable, elderly classicist, this university professor teased out of his speciality, gives us an unguarded document.

Le Roy wrote his book as an old man, in the last year of his

[1] Loys Le Roy, *De la vicissitude ou varieté des choses en l'univers et con-currence des armes et des lettres par les premieres et plus illustres nations du monde, depuis le temps ou a commencé la civilité & memoire humaine iusques à present* (Paris, 1575).

life, having just achieved his lifelong ambition of having
enough to eat—and to drink, if one is to believe Scaliger's
gossip.[2] Born in the Norman town of Coutances about 1510,
he was a poor boy whose talent was recognized at the local
cathedral school. He was probably recommended to the bishop,
who never resided in his diocese but who was, fortunately for
Le Roy, a man of culture who lived in Paris and moved about
in court circles.

In the 1520s it was possible to learn Greek in a small provincial town like Coutances; the vicar of the diocese, Guillaume de la Mare, may well have taught Le Roy before he
came to Paris. In any case Le Roy was soon in Paris, just in
time to take advantage of the lectures of the royal professors,
newly instituted by François I. He studied under Pierre
Danès and Jacques Toussain in company with other young
men soon to become famous scholars: Amyot, Dorat, and
Turnèbe. Through sheer talent, this young nobody from Nor-
mandy acquired first-class citizenship in the Republic of Letters; he became Professor Toussain's favorite student and since
Toussain himself had been Guillaume Budé's favorite disciple,
Le Roy had been opted in at the top. A glorious academic
career was open to him, but he was still poor.

How could a scholar live if he was not already a gentleman?
The surest way was to join the *robin* establishment, if possible.
With this end in view, Le Roy went off to Toulouse to earn a
law degree in November, 1535. Still penniless, he did, however, have the equivalent of a letter of credit in his possession:
a letter of recommendation from Guillaume Budé addressed to
the most likely patron in Toulouse, Jean de Pins, bishop of
Rieux. He spent four years in Toulouse, earning his degrees

---

[2] For the information in the next few paragraphs I am indebted to the scant
biographical chapter in A. H. Becker's *Loys Le Roy* (Paris, 1896), which
also provides a good bibliography of Le Roy's work. In addition to Becker's
monograph, there is the recent book by W. L. Gundersheimer, *The Life and
Works of L. Le Roy* (Geneva, 1966), which adds little to Becker but ought
to be consulted especially for its bibliography. See my review-essay devoted
to this book in *History and Theory* 7 (1968), pp. 151–158.

while serving as de Pins' secretary for his room and board. After the death of his employer, Le Roy returned to Paris and began his long and painful search for financial security.

Budé had just died. Le Roy wrote his biography and was advised to dedicate it to the chancellor, Guillaume Poyet. He did and was rewarded with a job at the chancellery. He followed the court in its travels and went abroad for official and other purposes. Always in need of money, he was handed on from one patron to the next within the European-wide *confrérie* of humanist intellectuals. In Turin he acted as secretary for François Errault, the president of the Turin *parlement*. He arrived in London with a letter from Cardinal Du Bellay to the royal councilor Paget and was presented to the king. In Paris he was helped by the jurist François Connan. Always hoping for royal favor, Le Roy translated the *Phaedo* which was read to the king. But he continued to starve. In the 1560s, two powerful patrons may have provided him with an *office* at the Paris *parlement*, but it was only in 1572 that he at last received a good appointment, as professor of Greek at the *Collège des deux Langues* to succeed Denis Lambin. Even this appointment—200 écus yearly—could not have assured him real security, for the salaries were always paid reluctantly and sometimes with delays as long as four years.

Le Roy's lifelong penury and his failure to penetrate very deeply into the comfortable world of the Parisian magistrates—despite his attractive credentials—is somewhat unusual, although in the absence of any systematic study of the Parisian *robins* as a social class, one cannot be sure. Whether his problem was politics, sex, or alcohol, there was one thing he was helpless against: he was born a little too soon. The real opportunities were not available before the 1560s. Bodin, about twenty years his junior, followed more or less the same route and had no trouble. In any case Le Roy was something of an outsider. His connection with Toussain and Budé, his law studies, his reputation as a philologist, all these were real enough credentials, but he had no stake in the establishment, and this shows in his book, as does his hunger and his bitterness.

"Rootless cosmopolitan" that he was, reluctantly free of many social comforts and pressures, he found it easier perhaps to think in terms of humanity, to study civilization instead of French civilization, to let his curiosity range more freely over wider fields. He was interested in industrial and military technology, in the techniques of farming, cattle raising, ship building, and clothmaking, in the details of wine production and of metal working; he saw the merits of Arab and Tartar society. Some of these interests would no doubt have receded into the background if he had become integrated, early in life, into the solid ranks of the magistrature. The *robins*, lively, intelligent, and broad-minded as they were, could not help taking their comfortable world as a model of right conduct. Their world was the courtroom and the book-lined study. Law, paperwork, and bureaucracy were the commonplaces of their life. Through the leaded windows of their studies and halls, history, no doubt, seemed at times to have existed only so as to create the *parlement*.

Predictably enough, the equivalent in Le Roy's book is the proposition that throughout history civilization rises to its most splendid heights whenever society is so arranged as to provide comfortable incomes for intellectuals. How else can one explain why civilization has not flourished uniformly or progressed evenly? "Men always have the ability to learn, as long as they are taught," Le Roy affirms. And yet, "there are certain illustrious ages, let us call them Heroïc Ages, when (political power and human knowledge going hand in hand) warfare, eloquence, philosophy, mathematics, medicine, music, poetry, architecture, painting, sculpture . . . all flourish together and together decline."[3] This happened repeatedly, in particular

---

[3] ". . . ains en certains ages illustres que pouvons appeler Heroïques, Esquelles (la puissance & sapience humaine s'entresuyvans) l'on a veu communément l'art militaire, l'eloquence, Philosophie, Mathematique, Medecine, Musique, Poesie, Architecture, Sculpture, Plastique Fleurir ensemble & ensemble dechoir." Le Roy, *Vicissitude*, p. 29.

among the Assyrians, Persians, and Greeks, later under Augustus and Trajan in Rome, among the Arabs, and again in his own time ("ce siècle" meaning roughly what we mean by "the Renaissance"). What causes such "take offs" in the history of civilization? The influence of the stars or the geographical setting may have something to do with it, he allows, but he always comes back to his favorite explanation: "the salaries offered to intellectuals."[4]

The frequency with which Le Roy returns to this pet thesis throughout the book is a weakness which will easily be excused. It is not a comic trait when it comes from the pen of this gifted Greek scholar who was still obsessed, in the last year of his life, with a pathetic desire to eat his fill. And his thesis is more than a case of special pleading; he poses the problem—and solves it—in a manner consistent with his entire historical method.

Thus his explanation of the origins of organized human society follows the same lines. Although his information is hardly recondite and although he has not done any real historical research, he manages to put together scraps from the Ancients with notes of contemporary travellers in such a way as to produce an entirely secular, plausible, and almost mechanistic account.

In the beginning "almost all the nations remained for a long time without letters." Of the books which we have, Le Roy reminds us, "there are none written more than three thousand years ago (except for the Hebrew books) and among the Gentiles there is no author more ancient than Homer." In guise of culture, these earliest societies had only an oral tradition. This is true of the American Indians, of the Hebrews before Moses

---

[4] "Or combien que se trouvent partout gens capables de sçavoir, pour veu qu'ils soient deument instituez; neantmoins il en y a de plus ingenieux & inventifs les uns que les autres, & plus aptes a certaines disciplines, ou par inclination naturelle & influence du ciel, ou par l'assiette du pais auquel ils naissent, ou par l'exercice qu'ils acoustument faire de jeunesse, ou par l'honneur nourrice des ars que lon faict & les loyers qui sont proposez aux scavans & expers." *Ibid.,* p. 28.

set their tradition down in writing, and of the Greeks before the
Homeric poems were written down.[5]

"The earliest men were very simple and brutal, hardly different from the beasts. They went about in the fields and mountains
eating the raw flesh of animals . . ." and greens growing wild in
the fields. Then, natural selection began the long mutation
which is human history: "As the stronger ones ate the best
foods, they lived longer," and "gradually men learned to make
their lives more comfortable. . . : they learned to cultivate ce-
reals, which until then had grown wild among the grasses and
the vine which also grew naturally . . . then they learned to
build, getting together in groups so as to live in greater security
and ease."[6]

Le Roy's economic determinism clearly does not stop with
his own desire to be paid: it is a fundamental way of explaining
history. Everywhere Le Roy sees evolution and everywhere it
is pushed on by economic challenges to which men respond.
At first, he contends, men ate each other, and then they began
to prefer other animals; at first men lived in a pastoral economy,
herding sheep and cattle, and then they turned to agriculture.
As their taste in food became more demanding, they were no
longer satisfied with milk and water and turned to artificial
beverages such as wine, beer, mead, and cider. At the same time
the evolution of their taste made them reject the simplest pot-
tery and turn to making cups of gold and silver, to cooling their
drinks with snow and ice, to preferring elaborate dining room
furniture to simple picnics on the grass.

The same process of refinement occurred in all materials and
crafts. The construction business and the textile industry provide Le Roy with a vast inventory of human progress. As production and the exchange of goods reached a certain stage, it
became necessary to trade further away, and the ship building
industry was born. Le Roy gives a small history of its progress

[5] *Ibid.*, p. 20.
[6] *Ibid.*, p. 25.

—from canoe to galleon—and examines the side products of maritime commerce: the growth of port towns, of arsenals, and of specialized professions to serve its needs. Like Bodin, Le Roy follows the growth of civilization through its various stages and finds that "as prosperity and leisure are achieved," the time has come for culture, "for need . . . taught men the arts necessary for survival," but, need once satisfied, they learned the arts "which serve pleasure."[7]

This kind of lofty generalization in the manner of Aristotle is Le Roy's favorite intellectual exercise; he is good at it, his examples seem fresh and well chosen, his reasoning seems original. Actually, when Le Roy gives this impression it is usually because he is translating or paraphrasing from the Greek; his originality is almost entirely due to his intellectual expatriation. No matter—his attempts at fitting the Heavenly City of the Greek philosophers into the contemporary world yielded something more important than new facts: new comparisons. Le Roy's unconscious expatriation worked like the deliberate *dépaysement* of the utopists and satirists. The voyages of his mind made him forget his first anchorage and enabled him to look at his own world like a stranger.

When does universal history begin? He examines the conflicting claims of the Indians, Ethiopians, Egyptians, Scythians, and Chaldeans. He cites the Jewish, Christian, and Islamic contention that God created the earth; the Greek myth of creation; and the Arabs' notion that they were created first. He pointedly reminds his readers of Augustine's denial, on theological grounds, of the existence of the antipodes and of their later discovery. "Leaving aside all the disputes and boasts of the various nations," Le Roy concludes, "all the fantasies and reasonings of the philosophers, we shall subscribe to the certitude of the Holy Scriptures on the question of the creation of

[7] "Donques entre tant de commoditez, croissant l'oysiveté avec l'opulence & ayse, ils s'appliquerent à l'estude des lettres"; "Premierement l'indigence . . . leur enseigna les ars necessaires à la vie, puis succederent ceux qui servent au plaisir. . . ." *Ibid.,* p. 27.

the world and of mankind. As for the story of civilization, which
is our subject, we will begin it with the Egyptians."[8] A quick
bow in the direction of the Sorbonne has not weakened his
point at all; on the contrary, he is clearly saying that the Creation, a subject about which historians and political scientists
know nothing, is one thing, and human history another. The
argument is familiar.

Universal history, then, as far as secular science is concerned,
begins with the first signs of civilization known to him, in
Egypt. Having settled this question, he moves on to the next
difficult theoretical issue: from this beginning, how does one
tell the story so as to achieve continuity and coherence? What
are the criteria for judging kingdoms? Which of them should
be singled out for detailed treatment, which should recede into
the background, which should be omitted entirely? How does
one compose an outline of history?

The amazing thing about Le Roy is that he has the answers.
When he is actually writing history, he is an incompetent and
uncritical compiler, but the theoretical parts of his book are
admirable. To the question, how does one judge a government?
the answer is, by the degree of its liberality toward intellectuals
and by the consequent flourishing of culture. That is how heroic
ages are created. Ptolemy Philadelphus in Egypt, Pericles in
Greece, the Arab rule under which so many great theologians
and scientists thrived, those were great moments in the history
of the world.[9] How do governments decline, how does the
culture of an age fall into ruin? The loss of liberty is the key
here; the glorious age of the Persians came to an end because
"they took too much of the people's freedom away and, intro-

---

[8] "Mais omises toutes telles disputes & vanteries des peuples, toutes fantaisies
& raisons humaines des philosophes, nous nous arresterons en la certitude de
l'escriture saincte touchant la creation du monde et du genre humain. Et
quant au discours des armes et des lettres dont il est icy question, y en-
trerons par les Egyptiens." *Ibid.*, p. 33.

[9] *Ibid.*, pp. 35–36, on Egyptian civilization; Book V on Greek civilization; and
Book VIII on Arab civilization.

ducing an authority more absolute than was suitable, they lost the friendship and the sympathy of the nation."[10]

Le Roy does not need to invent a scheme for telling the history of mankind—no need of four monarchies or seven ages or any other arbitrary arrangement. His theme is clear; he is telling the story of the rise and fall of civilizations. His single-minded and partisan absorption in this story leads him to a very useful and practical decision, namely, that the history of civilization is the only kind of universal history worth telling, the only kind historians *can* tell, anyway. The rest is literature—or theology.

In this new perspective, universal history is so vast, it includes so many nations and cultures, that the medieval patchwork technique of the translation of empires becomes hopelessly inadequate. At the same time, the exclusion of moralistic and prophetic forms of analysis in favor of a single criterion—the success and failure of civilization—also makes the task easier, at least at the high level of generalization chosen by Le Roy. Here the comparative method taken over from the jurists works wonders.

Civilization began among the Egyptians, Assyrians, and Persians. A specific region of the earth, the Near East, was singled out for the birth of human history. Since Le Roy is not concerned with theological issues, God's plan is irrelevant here. Was it mere accident, then, that the Near East served as the cradle of civilization? Le Roy does not believe in accident any more than Bodin does. In comparing these Near Eastern empires with each other, he finds that they all have certain things in common: they were very large, their governments were despotic, the climates favorable, and the populations servile. This combination of factors resulted in large revenues concentrated in a few hands. Here was the financial foundation of culture.

How did these civilized empires decline? Here again Le Roy

[10] *Ibid.*, p. 42.

provides a rational explanation: these empires were founded by capable men who were used to all hardships. "They supported hunger and thirst patiently, they drank water, they were skilled and practiced in the arts of war." Later, wealth, luxury, and civilization eventually sapped the rough virtues of these peoples; they became cowardly and voluptuous, victims of "the delights derived from excessive wealth."[11]

The comparative method can be applied to any historical topic. Thus, when Le Roy encounters religion and a clerical class in Egypt, he is moved to reflect that "at first men thought that religion was the only kind of knowledge possible" and that there were no intellectuals outside of the clergy. This state of affairs lasted for a long time and was common to most societies because religion was a necessary instrument of the state. That is why the clergy in every society have always been thought of as "first in authority, that is why they have been heaped with honors and well paid, that is why they—and their children—have been exempted from taxes and military service." Le Roy finds that this was true not only among the Egyptians and Assyrians, but also among the Hindus (Brahmins) and the Gauls (Druids), among the Greeks and Romans, and, of course, in Western Europe.

The same method can be applied to a study of the nobility; Egyptians, Persians, and Lacaedemonians, as well as the Arabs and the French, had a warrior class of hereditary noblemen who were not allowed to engage in trade and industry. This was also the case, in a somewhat different way, in Spain, Hungary, and Poland. In Turkish society, on the other hand, nobility was not a question of birth.[12]

Le Roy's method shapes his entire book, which is made up of intricate layers of comparisons. The topic of the first of the twelve chapters (or books) is "variety in nature." It is a worth-

[11] *Ibid.*, p. 47.
[12] *Ibid.*, pp. 48–50.

less little encyclopaedia of cosmological ideas and runs to some thirty pages. Its purpose, no doubt, was to show some sort of correspondence between the laws of nature and the laws of men, but Le Roy gets bogged down in astrological fiddle-faddle, the confusion compounded by his clumsy French.

The subject of the second chapter is "variety in language." Here Le Roy is on the solid ground of his own speciality. He shows how languages change, how some languages conquer others and spread over vast regions. The degree of culture of a people, the appeal of their religion, or the power of their armies can carry their language far beyond the borders of their country. The spread of Greek and Latin in antiquity, the later spread of Latin as the language of Christianity, the use of Hebrew and Arabic as sacred tongues, and the contemporary diffusion of Slavic languages, in Lithuania for instance, serve as examples. He also discusses the techniques of paper and ink manufacturing and the printing industry. In his conclusion he assimilates the laws which govern the life of languages to those which govern the life of civilization in general: "like buildings and clothes, like customs and folkways, like laws and magistrates, like the different ways of living in public or private, like weapons, machines and tools; thus words and languages die in the end, leaving nothing of themselves or their script as time goes on" (the languages of the Etruscans and the Carthaginians, for instance). Languages, like the civilizations which created them, are crude at first, then they become sophisticated as customs and culture become more refined, and finally they decline and perish.[13]

This short chapter (fourteen pages) is followed by an even shorter one (twelve pages) whose topic is the setting of civilization. Here he discusses prehistory and the causes of the growth of civilization. The fourth chapter is on Near Eastern civilization, the fifth on Greek civilization, and the sixth on Roman civilization. Chapter seven is a comparison of Roman civiliza-

---

[13] *Ibid.*, p. 21.

tion with other ancient civilizations, chapter eight is on Arab civilization, and chapter nine on other "nonwestern" cultures (Turks, Tartars, Mongols, Chinese, Indians, Abyssinians, Russians). Chapter ten, "Of the power, knowledge and excellence of this age," is a dissertation on the civilization of the Renaissance which he dates from about the middle of the fourteenth century. Chapter eleven is a comparison of Renaissance civilization with other heroic ages. The final chapter is an affirmation of progress; the Renaissance is the greatest of all heroic ages and it is not absolutely necessary that it, too, should decline.

In short, Le Roy's book is the first full-fledged example of the kind of general history which was to become popular in the eighteenth century. It is an essay on the spirit and customs of nations. All the elements of what would later become "philosophic history" are already here: the neglect of political and diplomatic history; the rationalist, secular tone; the high level of generalization; the ideological stand in favor of heroic ages when philosophers were kings—or at least honored and paid. Even the details are all here, such as the theory of the origins of the Renaissance which made it the direct result of the Turkish conquest of Constantinople, or the singling out of culture heroes (Copernicus, Pico della Mirandola), the interest in Mohammed and Islam, and the lyrical worship of novelty ("new lands, new customs, new kinds of men, mores, laws, folkways: new plants, trees, roots, liquors, fruits; new diseases and new remedies: new routes in the sky and on the ocean never tried before, new stars seen").[14]

Scholars could hardly have found anything new in Le Roy's book, which was above all a work of vulgarization, written in French to reach the court and the nobility. But it was more than that: it was also a dictionary of the ideas of the new avant-garde. No single item in this inventory of *salon* gossip and shoptalk could have raised an eyebrow in the Paris of the 1570s.

[14] *Ibid.,* pp. 115–116.

But, taken together, the entries make a surprising impression of tendentiousness and party spirit. Intended perhaps as a text-book, the *Vicissitude* was in reality a philosophic manifesto, the prototype of the encyclopaedic works of Bayle, Voltaire, and Diderot.

Already the characteristics of philosophic history can be clearly discerned. The break with theological history is com-plete. Embracing the whole world, delighting in non-Christian and exotic cultures, Le Roy ransacks the erudition of his time to provide illustrations for his philosophy of history. Emanci-pated from old dogmas, and lover of facts that he is, he is not, for all that, free from new dogmas. On the contrary, he proves how difficult it is to write universal history without a firm ideo-logical perspective.

Doctor Vignier's *Library*

Theoreticians like Bodin and Le Roy were not professional historians. The first was a jurist, the second a classicist. Neither had written any history from original sources. Nicolas Vignier, however, whom his colleagues referred to as *le docte Vignier*, was the most perfect specimen of the professional historian in his time.[1]

[1] For biographical information on Vignier one has to rely on a *Life of Vignier*, written by Guillaume Colletet and published as part of the fourth, posthumous volume of the *Bibliothèque historiale* (Paris, 1650). Colletet's *Life* also contains a listing of Vignier's works, but this information has to be

A contemporary of Bodin, that is, about twenty years younger than Le Roy, Vignier was born in 1530, the son of a wealthy *robin* in Bar-sur-Seine in the province of Champagne. He had all the advantages that Le Roy and Bodin spent their lives trying to acquire. His father was an important royal officer, the family one of the first families of this provincial town, safe in its titles and connections. Nicolas received an excellent classical education, studied law and medicine, and became a Protestant. He spent several years in exile in Germany with his wife and sons, practicing medicine and doing historical research. Finally, he returned to France, abjured, and was reinstated as a *robin* in good standing, although his wife and his sons stayed on in Germany and remained Protestant.

His career as an historian began officially with his return to France, although by his own testimony he had been working on his major *opus*, the *Bibliothèque historiale*, since the early 1560s. The first book he published was a Latin chronicle of Burgundy (Basel, 1575), but from the time of his return to Paris he wrote in French and concerned himself with the history of France and with the preparation of the *Bibliothèque historiale*. He held the appointment of historian and physician to King Henri III, and in 1589 he was named *conseiller d'etat*. His works on the history of France, on chronology, on the history of Brittany, and on church history are all erudite, competent, and original works. But the *Bibliothèque* (three gigantic folios published in Paris in 1588) sums up his aspirations and his researches on the subject of universal history.

Vignier is one of the very earliest representatives of the

---

used with caution. Pierre Bayle knew Vignier quite well. That is clear if one reads his *Dictionary* with this question in mind. See the article "Françoise," notes B and C, in the 1720 edition of Amsterdam, or the article "Radulphe" in the same edition. With the exception of the nineteenth-century biographical dictionary, *La France protestante,* compiled by the brothers Haag (who read Colletet's *Life* but were more interested in Vignier's son, who was a better Protestant than his father), modern reference works do not know Vignier. See the lamentable confusion in the entry "Vignier," *Dictionnaire des lettres françaises* (XVIe *siècle*), which could have been avoided simply by consulting the *Grand Larousse* (1876) which repeats the Haag information.

modern historical profession. Others before him had been awarded the title of royal historiographer and had been paid to write history. Yet, aside from the fact that most of these appointments had been nominal, taken seriously neither by the court nor by the appointee, official historiographers had been men of letters whose duties, if any, consisted of giving an elegant literary polish to the traditional body of chronicles.

Vignier expressly denied being a man of letters.[2] His appointment and the general respect he inspired show that the erudite *robins* were successfully imposing their new understanding of what history ought to be on French opinion. A great *robin*, Chancellor Michel de l'Hospital, had been the first to appoint a representative of the new breed of historical scholars to the office, the brilliant Protestant jurist François Hotman, but Hotman was prevented from exercising his duties by the civil war.

Vignier had nothing of the brilliance of Hotman. While he certainly participated in the general current of opinion which emanated from the law faculties of Bourges and Valence, and while he was sensible to the attractions of the *mos Gallicus*, he had probably not been subjected directly to the magnetic influence of Cujas as had so many of his friends and colleagues, for instance, Pithou or Pasquier. Moreover, if he was not already a pragmatist by nature, his legal and medical studies made him into one. His approach to historical problems was almost clinical. His fear of unfounded generalizations and his avoidance of theory come as a relief after the speculations of Bodin and Le Roy. Vignier is a man of facts. For him, universal history lacked the philosophical attraction it exerted on Bodin and Le Roy; he approached it in the spirit of a man who is going to put order in his house. The *Bibliothèque* is a huge spring-cleaning with no mercy for cobwebs.

The *Bibliothèque* is dedicated to King Henri III. Even in the dedication—this most conventional of literary forms—the royal historiographer shows that he looks upon his work in a

2 Vignier, *Sommaire,* Preface.

new way. In contrast to the resounding paeans of praise and
the far-fetched compliments to the royal dynasty usually found
in official works of this kind, Vignier's dedication seems very
sober and businesslike. His business is "la recherche & cognoissance de la verité de toutes choses." The use of history is
that "the mind goes forth, as it were, to travel through the
reading of good books & especially of histories in which, as in
a painted panorama, the things which happened in every region
of the earth will be represented: the vicissitudes of Fortune, the
praiseworthy qualities and those to blame in the customs of
men and nations; the origins, the progress and the evolution of
empires and kingdoms and the causes of their decadence and
ruin."

This is the classical and Renaissance philosophy of history
as the teacher of life, but with a very great difference. Men
can learn from the contemplation of their past, but not, as the
Ancients would have it, by turning history into a moral science,
not by modeling one's individual actions on those of a virtuous
hero of old, and not by studying the ways of Fortune so as to
learn to live with her. In Vignier's world Fortune does not exist
except as a metaphor. History is to be an instrument with
which to measure not the ways of Fortune, but the ways of men.

For Vignier the mechanism of history lies hidden in human
behavior itself. That is why *exempla* in the manner of Plutarch
no longer suffice. Excluding Fortune, divine providence, and
all other external determining forces (not as necessarily absent,
but as outside the historian's province), Vignier proceeds from
the theory already sketched out by Bodin and Le Roy to the
job at hand: to gather reliable facts for the eventual analyst
who will know how to make use of them. His work is different
in conception from the histories written in the classical manner.
It is also different from the universal histories in the Eusebian
manner, such as the German chronicles, because Vignier's
compendium is truly universal in scope and because it is entirely secular in spirit.

Vignier is not unaware of the originality of his book and he makes the point, quite clearly, that he is not writing a universal history in the traditional way: his book is a "work of a kind which, perhaps, has never been attempted . . . by anyone else, in any other language . . ." before, ". . . although some have written universal histories."[3]

His book is neither a political history in the classical manner nor an ecclesiastically oriented chronicle in the medieval manner: what is it then? In the preface to the first volume, Vignier tries to define his new kind of history. Under the title of *Historical Library*, he has gathered together "in lieu of universal history, in a summary and compendious fashion . . . all the most memorable and remarkable facts contained and dispersed in the various, innumerable and ample writings of all the historians and other writers who preceded us—sacred as well as profane—and in the Chronicles and Annals and . . . Monuments and Antiquities of all the nations" which he has been able "to get his hands on. . . ."

Having thus defined the scope of his sources, he goes on to define the scope of his interests; he is interested not only in the nature of "peoples, nations, cities, monarchies and republics but also in the nature of the religions," those religions whose origins and evolution "have been recorded by means of writing and historiography." He specifies, in other words, that he has no intention of writing about religions except where reliable documents are available for their *historical* study. He will treat both political and ecclesiastical history, but he does not stop there. In his search for total history, he will not leave out "other events happening at the same time in all the known and inhabitable parts of the earth," nor will he forget to narrate the history "of the arts, of the sciences and of literature. . . ."

While his book can be read as a compendium of general history, it is more specifically designed as a reference work for historians. Like the *Historical Library* compiled in antiquity

---

[3] These quotations are from the "Dedication to the King," unpaged, signed by Vignier in Paris, January, 1586, and printed at the head of the first volume of the *Bibliothèque historiale*.

by Diodorus of Sicily, Vignier's *Library* will be a *Guide to Historical Literature* in which all the historians will be cited with a précis of the subjects covered by their books and notes indicating the place and time when they wrote and in how many books and volumes their works were published.

Vignier intends to do much more than Diodorus. His method will be "to take a particular topic and to indicate the known sources for this topic, naming the author and the specific book and page on which the account can be found" and to show which account he prefers to follow "when there are conflicting sources" (*quand plusieurs ont diversement recité un mesme fait. . .*). Finally, "so that people won't think that I want them to believe what I write on my own authority," he will add the "reasons, the testimonies and authorities" on which he relies "on every point he touches, especially when he maintains some particular opinion which is different from that of others or when it is a matter of taking up and confirming some author's opinion or testimony or some passage or sentence which may appear doubtful or untrue; or when it is necessary to explain and clarify an obscure passage, to reconstruct and correct it if it is incomplete and corrupted, to set it straight if it conflicts with other sources."

Is this to say then that his book is intended only as a handbook? Is it to be a neutral tool for other historians and is Vignier to suppress his own judgment? Not at all. As could already be seen from his statement on his choice of sources and on the methods he employs to select these, Vignier intends not only to collect but also to criticize his sources.

He goes much further. His readers will not fail to notice, he writes in his preface, that he frequently goes out of his way to treat matters which he considers of greater importance "more amply than others. . . ." Indeed, one of the most useful things about his *Library*, he contends, is that students of history will be spared the task of reading a great deal of unimportant material, which he had had to wade through in order to prepare this digest. What they will find in his *Library* is the carefully calculated selection of the important and reliable sources, critically presented.

Vignier sums up his purpose as "the telling of the facts concerning all the nations in just measure according to their importance and merit and as he found them written by others." And to show that he is fully aware of the philosophical implications of his statements, he lashes out in self-defense and in advance against those who will hate this book: the ignorant, the know-nothings, and those who are blind to facts (Rabelais' Sorbonnistes, I should think); the simple-minded who read only contemporary history and have no interest in the past; the frivolous "sophists" who use history only to furnish them with a handful of epigrams for use in the *salons*; and, finally, the most dangerous, the Pyrrhonists, who deny that any historical knowledge is possible.

The preface promises a great deal. Those who knew Vignier —his books, his way of working, his horror of theories—must have been consumed with curiosity when the huge volumes of the *Library* came out and, having read the preface, they must have wondered how the learned Vignier hoped to avoid the difficulties inherent in his ambitious project. How could one write universal history without falling prey to the theoretical claptrap which marred all such undertakings, even the *Chronicle* of the erudite Melanchthon?

Vignier was clearly in difficulty. In the preface he bravely promises to avoid the errors of his predecessors: ". . . so far the subject has been handled by many dirty hands busy producing a heap of *Miroirs historiaux*, of *Mers des histoires*, of *Chronicles of chronicles*, of *Supplements of chronicles* . . . and other fiddle-faddle of the kind, full of errors of fact and ridiculous lies." How does Vignier propose to avoid these errors? In particular, how does he expect to arrange his facts? What ages, epochs, and periods will he use to make sense and order out of the immense *mutations* which had given his predecessors so much trouble?

Vignier hedges on this point. He is clearly uncomfortable. He does not seem to believe that any periodization is valid. Varro's solution, he writes in the preface, "seems less impertinent and more *à propos* than the systems of others who arrange history into ages and millenaries."[4] But he does not, for all that, adopt it.

Vignier devotes all of two pages of text to the period extending from the Creation to the Flood, which is roughly the equivalent of Varro's first age. The second age begins with Noah. To this period Vignier gives 176 pages. He has, however, too many misgivings about this arrangement: ". . . one should not imagine that this distinction of ages or epochs has been the same everywhere, in every country, among all peoples, cities and nations simultaneously; but rather, since some have had their beginnings and their end earlier or later than the others, the golden age or the iron age has ended in one place while beginning in another." With this in mind, Varro's simple rule of thumb becomes a convenient and obvious way of distinguishing between prehistory, folklore, and history in the development of any given society, but it cannot serve as an organizing principle of universal history. Even in its limited application it is not a scientific notion. It does not cover all cases, for the rise and fall of nations does not by any means always follow the same pattern. For an infinity of different reasons, Vignier realizes, a nation can degenerate or revive; prosperity corrupted the Greeks and the Romans, but servitude, poverty, and other afflictions as well as religious enthusiasm often regenerated nations, as was the case of the Spartans, of the Jews in captivity, or of the persecuted Christians, for instance.[5]

In the end even the small concession that Vignier makes to the theoreticians is taken back in practice. The third age never

4 "Quant à la distinction des temps & des siècles depuis la creation du monde, celle que Varro par le recit de Censorinus nous a donné . . . m'a semblé la moins impertinente & plus à propos que les autres qui les deduisent en aages & millenaires." Vignier, *Bibliothèque*, Preface.

5 *Ibid.*, I, p. 9.

materializes in the text of the *Library*. Other dutiful statements
are made in the preface but have no effect on the composition
of the book. He subscribes, in principle, to the Eusebian outline
of universal history in which the major distinction is between
the history of the Jews and the history of the second people of
God, the Christians, the epochal dividing point being, of course,
the first coming of Christ. But there is no trace of such a division in the text of the *Library*. Vignier is probably the first
Christian who can write universal history without seeing in
Christ an epochal event. On page 679 of the first volume, having reached the year of Christ's birth, Vignier devotes a page
to an erudite chronological discussion, but no epoch ends or
begins here. Twenty pages later Vignier has reached the year
of Christ's death; here again nothing happens, no epoch begins.
Instead, one finds a two-page critical essay on the historical
sources for this event, summed up in the following statement: "It would seem to be a point just about resolved among
the ancients of our religion (Tertullian, Lactantius and very
few others independent of them) that our Lord Jesus Christ
presented his body in sacrifice on the tree of the cross to re-
deem our sins. . . ."[6]

Is there no outline to Vignier's history then? Does he not
make good on his promise to digest all the raw materials of
history, to save the reader time, to emphasize the important and
to cut out the superfluous, to give each event and each nation
its due, to judge and arrange the history of the world? He does
do all this, but without reference to any of the traditional
schemes of periodization.

On the broadest level, history is organized into three periods:
the first, corresponding to the first volume, is antiquity. It
stretches from prehistory to the fall of the Roman empire (394

---

[6] "Il semble q̃ ce soit un point quasi tout resolu entre les anciẽs de nostre
religion (Tertullien, Lactance & bien peu d'autres separez) que nostre Seign.
Jesus Christ presenta son corps en sacrifice en l'arbre de la croix pour la
satisfaction de noz pechez. . . ." *Ibid.*, p. 697.

A.D.). The great bulk of the first volume is taken up with historical times proper (738 pages), but prehistoric times take up some 176 pages. Vignier explains his attitude toward folk traditions (those preserved in the Homeric poems, in the Old Testament, and in other "poetic" sources) in the preface to the first volume: "Such as they are, they give us, rather naïvely, a picture of that first antiquity." However, "as I publish these succinctly, just as I have found them in the most trustworthy and serious authors who have survived the general shipwreck of Antiquity, I will be satisfied if one accepts them for what they are worth, without investing them with more authority than is due, in the same spirit in which people who have discovered some antiquities hidden in the earth—statues or medals, coins or inscriptions—keep these finds and cherish them in their reverence of antiquity and by thinking about what these finds denote, although they are more than half crushed, broken, disfigured or consumed by rust."

The period covered by the second volume (394 A.D. to 1094 A.D.) is what we would call the early Middle Ages; it is the history, as Vignier puts it, of the nations which arose out of the ruins of the Roman empire—including the history of the Arabs. Vignier, like Bodin and Le Roy, is interested above all in the history of civilization and he shares the humanist and Protestant distaste for the Dark Ages. It is natural that he should treat Islamic civilization in detail and just as natural that he should evince little interest in the narration of feudal *melées* and saints' lives which make up so much of Western history in those centuries. Still, he certainly goes too far for the taste of some of his contemporaries; in this volume, in which events are dated from the year of the Hegira (beginning on page 255), there is not a single saint in the index.

There is no radical break between the second volume and the third, which begins with the Crusades and ends with Magellan's circumnavigation of the earth (1095–1519), "for the subjects of these two volumes are intimately connected with each other," Vignier explains.[7] Still the third volume has its own important and new themes, principally that of European expansion and of the rise of Renaissance civilization.

There are three periods, then: antiquity, the Middle Ages, and modern times. This division is a purely pragmatic one. There is no implication of laws governing history; his periods are not assigned specific moral qualities in the old-fashioned manner. The distinction between one period and the next is a very fragile one. Vignier emphasizes the continuity of history; he subscribes to no catastrophic theories. "The disintegration of one thing is the generation of another and vice-versa," he explains.[8] Thus, the ruin of the Romans was at the same time the birth of new nations, and the great achievements of modern times had their roots in the Middle Ages.[9]

This perspective on world history has changed remarkably little since the sixteenth century. In the course of the last three hundred years or so, books on universal history written by scholars—accredited members of the international humanist *confrérie*—have, most of them, reflected the humanist, nationalist, and progressivist views first given currency by the erudite treatises of the Parisian *robins*. One has to allow, of course, for some variations—German nationalism instead of French, the preoccupations of a Benedictine prior or a German professor instead of those of a French court physician—but, taken as a whole, the modern outlook on the shape of universal history was born.

Historical research now stood emancipated from theology, and its task was clearly defined as the reconstruction of all

[7] *Ibid.*, III, Preface.

[8] *Ibid.*, II, Preface.

[9] A fourth volume of the *Bibliothèque historiale* was published some fifty years after Vignier's death (Paris, 1650). This volume runs to only 155 pages of text said to be printed from Vignier's manuscripts, which may be true. The period covered is that from the election of Charles V to the death of Melanchthon (1519–1560). This volume also contains Colletet's *Life* and 95 pages of corrections and additions to the entire work.

past events for which reliable sources existed. Universality had acquired a new meaning. All human activities were worth investigating and in every known region of the earth. The ancient primacy of Mediterranean politics and the medieval primacy of Christian church affairs as historical subjects were both superseded, and the old meaning of universality, conceived as the duty to account for all the years since Creation, was abandoned to the theologians.

Vignier's beliefs, or doubts, concerning the Creation were irrelevant to his functions as an historian. It did not matter how many thousands of years the earth or mankind had existed before the creation of the earliest historical documents, for in Vignier's view history proper began only then, and the historian could not make professional pronouncements about the *spatium incognitum* which stretched out beyond. Within the *spatium historicum* for which Vignier accepted responsibility, however, he conceived of no theoretical limits to the direction of his inquiries. Whatever could be documented was a fitting subject for the historian. He proceeds on the assumption that his reader will want to know not only about politics but also about religion and culture. The most striking result of this policy is that the history of religion is taken over by the historian and treated in as objective a fashion as politics. Twenty years earlier, Bodin had expelled church history from the historian's domain in order to free him from a theological interpretation of events. Now we have come full circle, for Vignier takes over church history and treats it exactly as if it were profane history. He has secularized the history of religion itself.

He assumes responsibility for telling *that which is historically demonstrable* in the history of religion. He gives the history of the various councils and synods and, in effect, shows that the Christian church has been subject to the same *mutation* which affects all human history. This theme is taken over, no doubt, from the Protestant church histories, but without their doctrinal conclusion. Vignier does not say, as do the Protestant theologians, that the *mutations* of the church since the time of Christ are errors caused by Satan, or that Christians must return to the true doctrine of the primitive church—of the time, that is, before the *mutations* began. He merely shows that the church as an institution has changed in the course of time, as have all other institutions.[10]

His interest in church history is not limited to the treatment of clerical institutions. He is also interested in the history of theology and, above all, in the history of heresy. The origins of Protestantism are an important topic in his book. Whenever he can find any evidence, he notes rebellions against orthodox doctrine. In the year 1105 A.D., for instance, he notices that "under Bruno, archbishop of Trèves, four men were expelled from the diocese and declared heretics" because they denied the doctrine of transubstantiation and infant baptism and spoke against the authority of the Church of Rome. In 1122 "There were men in Germany who spoke and wrote against pilgrimages, pardons and indulgences."[11]

The history of culture occupies a large place in the *Library*. Here, also, Vignier's feeling for evolution, his talent for making generalizations, and his love of original sources combine to make *historia scholastica* into something quite different from the usual humanist catalogue of illustrious men.

A good example of his method can be found in the cultural rubric of the year 1129. After brief mentions of Honorius, bishop of Autun, "a man learned in all the liberal arts and sciences & an excellent historian," and Ordericus Vitalis, "an

---

[10] Vignier states clearly on the first page of the preface to the first volume that religions will be treated like nations or cities. He will describe from available historical sources their "origins, progress, evolution, decline . . . the changes, transformations, incidents. . . ." Compare this with the medieval outlook still preserved by Bossuet a hundred years later: "Here then is religion, always uniform, or rather always the same since the beginning of the world. . . ." *Discours sur l'histoire universelle* (Paris, 1681), in the Gallimard Pleiade edition (Paris, 1961), p. 765. Klempt, *Säkularisierung*, p. 49, is obviously quite wrong when he attributes the first attempt at the secularization of ecclesiastical history to Cellarius (1685).

[11] Vignier, *Bibliothèque*, III, pp. 26, 59.

English priest who very likely lived about that time and who wrote an Ecclesiastical History which has not yet been printed" (but whose manuscript he saw in the hands of Monsieur de La Croix du Maine), Vignier turns to the subject of medieval philosophy: "Jean Rouzelin or Roucelin," he writes, "a native of Brittany and a great philosopher," lived at that time. He may well have been the inventor of the "new manner of philosophizing and disputing of philosophic matters based on the doctrine of Aristotle." This new philosophic method "which treated of all matters and reduced them to questions for debate . . ." was so well suited to the needs of all the intellectuals of the time "that it was very quickly adopted and practiced in the schools not only in the field of profane philosophy but also in theology" and in medicine, law, and grammar as well. According to Otto of Freising, Vignier notes, Rozelin was the inventor of the new science. But Peter Abelard claims that he invented it. At this point Vignier gives us a long quotation from Abelard and then continues his exposition by describing the controversy between nominalists and realists, "two philosophical factions" (comparable, he points out, "to the factions in a civil war or to the conflict between Guelfs and Ghibelines") "which have kept all the schools and universities of Europe busy for something like three hundred years."[12]

In addition to the three well-defined subjects which take up most of the space—politics, religion, and culture—there are other facts worth including which defy classification, the history of explorations, for instance. Vignier carefully notes the long-range plans for the exploration of the African coast by the Portuguese (1480), the colonization of the Canary Islands (1483), the Portuguese mission to Ethiopia (1484), further Portuguese expeditions (1487), and Columbus' discoveries

[12] *Ibid.*, pp. 72–73. As a rule Vignier likes to give generous extracts from primary sources, as when he quotes Abelard on his own life or William of Malmesbury on the First Crusade. When he is following a secondary source, on the other hand, his usual practice is to give a very brief précis of his source and to direct the reader to the book he has used.

(1492). From then on hardly a year goes by without news of explorations right up to the last entry in the *Library*, which is Magellan's voyage.

The inclusion of cultural and religious history—and of other matters, such as the history of exploration, of invention, and of technology—is one measure of the *Library*'s universality. Another is its truly global scope.[13] To the major countries of Western and Mediterranean Europe normally included in the field of vision of European historians, Vignier systematically adds Scandinavia and Eastern Europe. His curiosity does not stop there; not only the Turks but also the Russians enter the picture. Tartar raids beyond the Volga River are duly recorded. The Arabs in Granada and in North Africa do not escape his attention. Here, too, although his knowledge is necessarily thin and although he depends entirely on secondary authorities—always carefully cited—Vignier tries to see large currents developing over the years. Thus one of the larger themes of the third volume is the rise of the Russian empire ("commencement du recouvrement de la liberté des Princes de Moscovie"), which he considers an important enough development to add another foundation date to his multiple chronology—the years from the foundation of the Russian empire, which take their place side by side with the years from Christ and the years from the Hegira.

There are usually good reasons for Vignier's emphases; his interest in early heresies and his entire view of church history are colored by his Gallican and even Protestant leanings, and his interest in Eastern Europe owes something, no doubt, to the fact that his royal patron, Henri III, was also briefly king of Poland. These special interests take nothing away from the fundamental and consistent universality of his method. The only real limitation imposed on this ambitious project was the lack of sources, a very serious limitation indeed. The novelty

---

[13] Excepting, of course, those lands which were as yet unknown or little known to European scholars, China in particular.

and originality of his book lie almost entirely in the way he puts information together, for outside of his special field, the history of France, Vignier works for the most part with secondary sources.[14]

By emphasizing, as I have done, Vignier's will to overcome the lack of sources, his historical intelligence at work behind the colorless entries which pile up year after year in the endless pages of his book, I may have misled the reader into thinking of the *Bibliothèque historiale* as a sensational, lively, or at least interesting book. I am afraid it is not even interesting, except to the specialist student of the history of historiography.

The total history Vignier desired was an ideal so far removed from his reach that he had to content himself with writing a *Guide to Sources* instead. It is only occasionally in the course of this reference work that the sources enable Vignier to rise above bibliography and to write history. The prefaces are in some ways the most interesting parts of his *Library*. There his assumptions about the nature of history are stated explicitly, in particular his conviction that history must be both general in scope and founded on primary sources.[15]

These two fundamental aims, however, could rarely be reconciled in practice. The historian who set out, as Vignier wished to do, to reconstruct the entire past of mankind had to put his trust, most of the time, in secondary compilations of doubtful value. Much of the time he lacked even those and could, in all honesty, do no more than record the extent of his ignorance.

These very great obstacles standing in the way of the historian did not discourage Vignier. He despised the position of the skeptics. In his opinion there was a sufficient fund of evi-

14 Which may account for Scaliger's cranky judgment: "Vignerius bonus in Historia Gallica, in caeteris nil." *Scaligerana* (Amsterdam, 1740), II, p. 614.

15 On primary sources and their importance, see the foreword, "Au Lecteur," in *Sommaire*. On the need for general history see especially the preface to the first volume of the *Bibliothèque*.

dence buried in the existing records to make reasonable, if modest, judgments about the past.[16] To be sure, there were enormous lacunae and discrepancies in the sources, but patient work could uncover more evidence and resolve some of the worst discrepancies. Furthermore, if the eventual result should fall short of perfection, if the historians could only vouch for approximate truths, he would settle for this.

[16] ". . . quelque diversité ou repugnance qu'il y ait entre les Chronographes et Historiographes . . . toutefois pour cela n'a pas été toute la verité ensevelie, ains on peut tirer assez pour satisfaire au gout d'un jugement sain et modeste. . . ." Vignier, *Bibliothèque,* I, Preface.

La Popelinière:
the representation
of everything

Eighth chapter

In Vignier's *Library* the shape of the new history to come can be glimpsed here and there, but for a detailed blueprint one has to turn to La Popelinière's *Idea of Perfect History*, published some ten years later. This book and its companions, the *History of Histories* and the *Project for the New History of the French*, summed up the historical thought of an entire generation.

La Popelinière was born on a country estate on the eastern edge of Poitou in 1541. Like Bodin, Le Roy, Pasquier, and so many others, he received a good classical education in Paris and studied—law, presumably—at the University of Toulouse. As a younger son, destined at first for a career in the royal administration—in the church, one would have said only a generation earlier—he found himself propelled into the military because of his older brother's death. He commanded infantry and naval task forces in the Huguenot armies; after some unpleasant experiences with the fortunes of war and with superior officers, he returned to a life of scholarship.[1] Among his early books were translations of works on the art of war and on geography, but his main interest at first was contemporary history. His *History of France* was admired and copied. In it he wrestled with the problem of recounting the events of the civil wars with scrupulous objectivity and accuracy.[2] The question of just what happened and exactly where and when in the course of the confusing battles and political crises of his time was difficult enough. La Popelinière shared the views of men like Bodin, Pasquier, and Vignier; the events he was witnessing were the product of history and in order to understand them he would have to pursue the causes of the civil wars far into the past of the French nation. "I start my history way back, before the beginning of the civil wars," he explains at the start of his *History of France*. "There would be little profit and even less pleasure in describing the wars waged by Charles V and his son Philip against the Kings of France—or the great religious revolution within the Christian world and the civil wars which

[1] See the biographical notice at the beginning of his *Histoire de France*, vol. I. The scant evidence for a biography of La Popelinière has been assembled by George Wylie Sypher, "La Popelinière, Historian and Historiographer" (Ph.D. diss., Cornell University, 1961).

[2] La Popelinière's history of the civil wars appeared in a first version as *La vraye et entière histoire de ces derniers troubles* in Cologne (1571), Basel (1572), and La Rochelle (1573). These early narratives were so successful that they were simply cleaned up for Catholic consumption and republished in 1581 under the title of *Histoire de France* by a team of plagiarists. La Popelinière himself published a definitive version, also under the title of *Histoire de France*.

ensued—if this were done in a dry-as-dust manner, leaving the sources and the evolution of the hostilities between these monarchs unexplained and the origin and progress of the Reformation a mystery." In order to discover the origins of these events, he naturally read the older histories, and discovered that they were of very little use to him. He was forced to start from scratch, because the older histories were nothing but raw, unevaluated data. "To understand history is not to remember facts and events," he explains. "The essence of a work of history lies in the knowledge of the motives and true causes of these facts and happenings. There is little use in a fact—even if it is truly and simply reported—if the cause is lacking or the means by which it was brought about. And yet that is all we can get from the histories available to us."[3]

Some twenty-five years later he expanded these judgments into a full-scale survey of the history of historiography. In this *History of Histories* he offered a consistent critique of past historians and developed a theory of historiography linked to a more general theory of civilization.

In its most primitive form, La Popelinière argues, history was to be found everywhere, in the form of songs, dances, symbols, and other mnemonic devices. This earliest form of historiography is typical of primitive societies, when men were "ruraux & noncivilisez." "For there never was a nation—before or after the invention of letters—which did not in some fashion retain the memory of some notable deeds in the form of songs, proverbs or folk tales [*chants, devis ordinaires & bruits communs*]." And "some say that the songs of Homer were conserved in this manner."[4] The Germans according to Tacitus, the Gauls

---

[3] La Popelinière, *Histoire de France,* I, pp. 3–4.

[4] La Popelinière, *Histoire des histoires,* p. 27. This volume contains not only the work entitled *Histoire des histoires* itself, but also two treatises, *Idée de l'histoire accomplie,* and *Dessein de l'histoire nouvelle des françois.* These three works will be cited as *Histoire des histoires, Idée,* and *Dessein,* respectively. The only published study of La Popelinière's theoretical works, aside

according to Caesar, the Africans and Americans according to
contemporary evidence all possessed this kind of tribal tradition.[5] Everywhere in the world, runs La Popelinière's thesis,
history began in the same way.[6]

This earliest kind of historical tradition, which he calls
natural history, was transformed, wherever writing was introduced, into a second kind of historiography, which he calls
poetic history. No longer as natural as folk tradition, poetic
history is often deliberate and self-conscious: the oracles of the
Greek sibyls, the Hebrew prophecies, and the early Roman
songs are examples.[7] A third stage in the development of historiography is reached when prose records are kept of the most
notable events. This annalistic literature could be found, for instance, among the Hebrews, Assyrians, Persians, Arabs, Greeks,
and Romans.[8] Finally, historiography reaches a fourth stage,
a true maturity, with Herodotus.[9]

The general conclusion of La Popelinière's historiographical
studies was that no noticeable progress had been made since
Herodotus in the science of history. This did not mean that the
discipline had been perfected, once and for all, by the Greeks.
It meant only that the achievement of Herodotus was followed
by two thousand years of stagnation. Not only was there room
for progress, but La Popelinière went so far as to suggest that
what the Ancients had done was hardly history at all.

In his treatise, *The Idea of Perfect History*, he tried to de-

---

from my general essay, "The Renaissance Background of Historicism," *History and Theory* 5 (1965), pp. 48–60, is Myriam Yardeni's "La conception
de l'histoire."

[5] La Popelinière, *Histoire des histoires*, pp. 28–30.

[6] "Ainsi fut la première source de l'histoire semblable de substance entre tous
les peuples anciens. . . ." *Ibid.*, p. 33.

[7] *Ibid.*, pp. 39–40.

[8] *Ibid.*, p. 158.

[9] *Ibid.*, pp. 67–68.

fine his own ideal of what proper history should be. The first requirement of this future history is that it should be *general*: "l'Histoire digne de ce nom doit estre generale."[10] None of the ancient or medieval historians met this requirement. As La Popelinière saw it, the New History he was advocating and whose main feature was to be its universality had not yet come into existence. He singled out the work of Vignier as the most advanced published so far,[11] and he observed that among his contemporaries there was a sizable group of scholars working in the right direction and preparing the advent of the New History,[12] but the goal had not been reached yet. For his part, he was not ready to write his New History of France. For the moment, he thought it advisable to outline the theoretical problems facing him—and future historians—in this task.

La Popelinière indicts all past historiography on several counts, but what concerns us here is his criticism of the philosophical failure of all past historians, namely of their failure to write *general* history. What does he mean by general history? In particular, what is the relationship between general history as he understands it and the Christian idea of universal history?

Like Vignier, La Popelinière ignores the Christian theories of universal history. History is not determined by any outside forces, at least none amenable to observation by the historian. The notion that all history is the history of degeneration, La Popelinière refutes explicitly, as Bodin had done before him.[13] Unlike Bodin, he feels no great need to replace old deterministic theories with new ones. He does not share Bodin's enthusiasm for the notion that there are hidden laws governing

[10] La Popelinière, *Idée,* p. 97.

[11] ". . . lequel plus docte, plus curieux et moins passioné que tous ses devanciers. . . ." La Popelinière, *Dessein,* p. 350.

[12] In the preface to La Popelinière, *La vraye et entiere histoire* (Basel, 1572).

[13] La Popelinière, *Idée,* p. 3.

the course of human history, laws which would eventually be discovered by the social scientist.[14] He knows of no such laws, except that the diversity of time and matter is such that gradually everything changes among men.[15]

The phrase "universal history" has lost all metaphysical connotations. For La Popelinière, as for Vignier, it is synonymous with general history,[16] but, at the same time, and this seems to me a point of overriding importance, "'general history" is not a neutral phrase. On the contrary, it is a phrase charged with emotional commitment. (As *histoire universelle* in the eighteenth century and as *Weltgeschichte* in the nineteenth, it was destined for a sensational career.) La Popelinière needs hundreds of pages to define general history and even then does not quite succeed. The problem had worried Bodin, Le Roy, Vignier, and many others. It was the chief philosophical problem faced by the new generation of erudite historians. Shunning the old theological interpretation of the meaning of human history as an exercise outside of their field of competence, they were sometimes content to cite Cicero or Polybius instead and leave it at that. But ancient views on the nature of history had very little actual relevance to the vision of the past which was emerging out of the historical researches of men like Vignier and Pasquier, and La Popelinière saw this very clearly.

The most radical difference, as he saw it, was that the Ancients, in principle, could only write contemporary history. Aside from a very few exceptions (Varro), "their knowledge was only common knowledge, that is to say, information about their own time [*un savoir commun, voire des choses de leur temps*]." Bound by the convention according to which the historian could only write about affairs he himself observed directly or through interviews with eyewitnesses, the Ancients

[14] Bodin's efforts in this direction he characterizes as "curieuses recherches fort eloignées de la connaissance et actions des hommes." *Idée*, p. 29.

[15] *Ibid.*, p. 283.

[16] *Ibid.*, p. 82.

could never rise to the level of general history. And yet, "what matters is to write a worthy general history," and this would be impossible if the historian had to limit himself to events he could observe. "Under those conditions you would always be ignorant of the past"; instead of general history, "you would only have particular histories which would give you information only about events which occurred in the writer's presence."[17]

The sum of particular histories does not make up general history. Why not? Because La Popelinière is not using "general" or "universal" in the common-sense meaning of these words. The universality of history is more than a matter of scope for him. The issue is not whether the historian chooses to write about a period of thirty years or three thousand. What he means by generality or universality is a method inherent in the historian's approach to his subject. The subject, in fact, can be almost anything; it is the treatment which makes history universal.[18]

No matter what their subjects were, the ancient historians had almost never risen above *simple* history. Neither Xenophon's account of an expedition nor Thucydides' narrative of a war, La Popelinière claims, can give the reader "an understanding of the Greek way of life," "for he cannot, from those accounts, reach an understanding of the foundations of the Greek state, or find out about their officers and magistrates, their religion, their laws, their way of life [*moeurs*] and, in general, the nature of Greek society [*la Police des Grecs*]." When you take up a Greek or Roman history book, invariably, says La Popelinière, you end up putting it down with an unsatisfied feeling after reading it through. You know that there is something lacking. Somehow you expect more from historians.

"Why should Thucydides' book merit the name of history

---

[17] *Ibid.,* p. 27.

[18] ". . . l'Histoire sera Generale, quãd l'autheur luy aura donné la substance entiere & accomplie des Estats qu'il veut representer." *Ibid.,* p. 85.

more so than a narrative of the French civil wars does?" asks La Popelinière. Both are examples of simple history. He is inclined to put this kind of historical work in the same category with "annals, diaries, journals, memoirs, commentaries, etc." as the raw materials which would eventually serve in the composition of general history ("qui ne doyvent servir à l'Histoire que de matière pour y dresser un Narré accomplis").[19] As such—as primary sources, we would say—these simple histories are indispensable "because true history is founded on things seen or things one has read, seen, or heard, that is to say, of events contemporary with the person who is describing them."[20] These simple histories, however valuable as sources, should not be confused with general history.

Simple history is always incomplete, this much is clear. "Thus, Thucydides, Xenophon, Sallust and their kind wrote not the history of Greece or Rome, but rather a particular discourse on the Athenians, or Catilina or Juggurta." All these histories are concerned exclusively with one or, at best, a few aspects of life, usually politics and warfare. This arbitrary narrowness makes nonsense out of their historical vision; "it is as if someone, intending to write the history of France or of some other country, chose to write only about the condition of the nobility or of the clergy; one could hardly say that he succeeded in picturing the condition of France."

True history must be complete. It must include "the character, the mores [*moeurs*], the customs [*coustumes*], and the way of life [*façons de faire*] of the people in question."[21] Every aspect of life that can be documented must enter the historian's vision. What is more, the historian ought to be calling the shots. Far from being satisfied with a passive role, the historian should

---

[19] *Ibid.*, pp. 93–96.

[20] "Pour ce que la vraye Histoire se dresse des choses veues, ou qu'on a peu lire, voir & entēdre. C'est à dire, des accidens survenus au temps de celuy qui les descrit." *Ibid.*, p. 40.

[21] *Ibid.*, p. 95.

not accept the version of events left by contemporaries. They did not know what was important. For example, "who among the ancients told us about the regions out of which the Franks came? or about those through which they passed on their way into Gaul? Did they tell us about the mores, the laws, the institutions, the officers of the Franks? Or even whether they had kings, and if so, how the kings were instituted?" La Popelinière has an arsenal of important questions for general history, and none of the Ancients saw fit to answer them. About early French history, he wants to know "what was the power of the monarchy? What were the honors, the powers and the rights of clerics? and of noblemen, of magistrates, of financiers and other estates?" In all these matters,

> . . . what were the differences between Gauls, Romans and Germans in Gaul? What difference between Franks and Germans? When, how and by whom was the Christian religion introduced, received, augmented, resisted, implanted in Gaul among peoples of such variegated temperaments? What was the origin and the progress, what were the changes and the reforms and the variations of ecclesiastical discipline? . . . By what laws, customs, way of life [*forme de vivre*] and of justice, by what institutions in peace and in war did these peoples [the alien Franks, Germans, and Romans whom he opposed to his native ancestors, the Gauls] manage to stay on in the face of the deplorable patience of our old fathers [the Gauls]? If you are not quite clear and straight in all these matters, what knowledge can you claim to have of the condition of the French? What history could you write about their country and their actions?[22]

General history, in short, ought to be "the representation of everything."[23] Simple history is not only incomplete, it is misdirected. The difference between the two, as La Popelinière defines it, is very close to the distinction twentieth-century philosophers like Croce and Collingwood make between chronicle

[22] La Popelinière, *Dessein,* p. 352.
[23] La Popelinière, *Idée,* p. 85.

and history. "There is the greatest difference," writes La Pope-linière, "between the act of searching for and, by various rea-sonings, at last discovering the truth, and, on the other hand, simply reciting the cause and motive of some project or event."[24]

Here we have it, at last. The most distinct characteristic of general history will be its philosophical emancipation from the chaos of events. Bodin had fought the battle against the feeble tyranny of the old interpretation of universal history. Since then, the gravest threat to the historians' peace of mind had turned out to be the terrifying anarchy of facts. The record-keeping of the old historians—more or less intelligent, in-formed, and impartial—was shaped by the events, was nothing but an echo of the events and, consequently, almost meaning-less. The task of general history was to transmute these raw facts into meaning, to elevate history to a philosophy.

For La Popelinière, and for the French historical school in general, universal history (*histoire universelle, générale, ac-complie; historia integra, iusta, perfecta, consummata*) was to be a method for reconstructing the past and making sense out of it. On this much the most theoretical-minded (Bodin) could agree with the most pragmatic (Vignier).

How certain the conclusions of the universal historian could ever be and, consequently, how clear the meaning of universal history could ever become were other questions and hotly de-bated ones. La Popelinière summed up the arguments in this debate in his *Idea of Perfect History*. He himself wavered on

---

24 ". . . il y a grande différence de rechercher & par divers raisonnemens des-couvrir en fin la Verité des choses: & reciter simplement la cause & motif de quelque dessein ou accidens." *Ibid.,* p. 103. Compare this with Collingwood's phrasing of the same distinction: "It is the difference between the recorder of those facts which happen to be directly visible from his own empirical situation in history, and the thinker who, defying the empirical limitations of time and place, claims for himself, in principle, the power to recount the whole infinite history of the universe; restricting himself to this part of it or that not because he happens to be planted there, but because it is his own good pleasure so to restrict himself." *Speculum Mentis,* p. 204.

these questions, as was only natural. On the one hand, the conception of perfect history implies that there is in reality a meaning in history, for perfect history is that ideal achievement of historical research, namely the full discovery of the secretly well-ordered past.[25] On the other hand, perfect history is, after all, only an ideal: one may come close to it, but it will never be completely achieved.[26]

In the first place there are all the difficulties inherent in the nature of the sources: "how can you ever form an opinion in the face of so much diversity, so many writers describing the same event in as many different ways?"[27] These difficulties must be faced squarely; there is no use being overawed by them. To be sure, the historian has his moments of weakness. La Popelinière himself admits that he often wished he did not have to reach a conclusion. As he composed his history of the civil wars, he was often tempted to suspend judgment in the hope that sooner or later those issues which seemed confused to him would be cleared up. Not that he was attracted by the Skeptics. He merely wished he could avoid describing publicly, as facts, events of which he could not be sure. Really, he wished he could just hold on to his conjectures to see whether, in time, they would be confirmed or not.[28]

But certainty is not to be hoped for in historical demonstrations; as soon as this fundamental fact is grasped, the going

[25] In an early work, La Popelinière expressed his conviction that ". . . les causes des accidens humains s'entretiennent d'un lien eternel et connu de peu de gens. . . ." *Histoire de France,* p. 4.

[26] La Popelinière, *Idée,* p. 35.

[27] "A quelle opinion vous arresterez vous en si grande diversité d'avis autant que d'Autheurs qui parlent tousiours diversement d'une mesme chose?" La Popelinière, *La vraye et entiere histoire,* p. 4r.

[28] ". . . i'ay souvent doubté à quoy ie me pourrois resoudre. Non que ie voulousse tenir en fief de la vieille ou nouvelle Academie: non plus que me conformer a ceux qui trop foibles à se resoudre suspendoient leur advis en toutes choses: moins encor m'assubiectir aux tousiours douteuses considerations des sceptiques & Pirrhoniens: ains seulement pour voir si la suitte du temps & la conference des gens de merite confirmeroient ou renverseroient mes premieres conceptions." La Popelinière, *Histoire des histoires,* p. 6.

gets easier. One should expect no more than "arguments so probable as to persuade the reader that the historian's version of events is at least the most plausible: with the understanding that his version can be changed if one can come up with—and prove—a more convincing hypothesis."[29]

There is such a thing as an historical method, after all. First of all, one must ask whether the text in question really was written by the man to whom it is attributed. If so, then what was the author's country and religion? When was he writing and under what government? What were his sources of information? Under what circumstances did he compose the text? Did he receive patronage of any sort? How much time did he spend writing his account? Does his version of events conform to that of his predecessors and successors? Has it been disputed? If so, in what particulars and by whom?

Of course, even the greatest precautions, the most thorough control of the sources, cannot guard one against the subjectivity of the historian himself. "The early Greeks and Romans certainly never spoke as the later Greek and Roman historians make them speak. Nor was their way of life such as the historians have them describe. The classical historians, for the most part, do not represent the civilization of their ancestors as it really had been, but rather in the image of their own times. An old mistake this, and one of which we have never been free."[30]

In spite of these difficulties, the knowledge of the past is possible if only one decides—against the opinion of those who will believe nothing unless they have absolute certainty—to speak

---

29 ". . . arguments si probables, qu'on y soit atiré sinon a le suivre du moins a se le persuader pour vray semblable. Avec dessein de le changer si on faict preuve de chose meilleure." La Popelinière, *Idée*, p. 317.

30 "Car il est certain, que tãt les premiers que secõds Grecs & Romains, ne parlerent iamais come les Historiens Grecs & Latins qui les ont suivy les font parler. Ny les façõs des moeurs, des tẽps & affaires, estoient telles qu'il les leur font raconter. Car ils les representes la pluspart telles qu'elles estoient, non selon le temps & moeurs anciennes: mais selon le siècle de celuy qui les recite. Faute ancienne, & qui a tousiours esté continuée iusques icy." *Ibid.*, p. 76.

of the past by means of conjectures as plausible and as close to the truth as possible. With this modest result in mind, the reader will find it worth his while to follow the historian's labors. For the end result is the deduction of the course of human experience, "from century to century, along something like a continuous thread, right up to the present."[31] And this "continuous" or "general" history, such as it is, comes as close as is possible to the discovery of the meaning of the human condition. Its results will never be certain. Nevertheless, for La Popelinière and his colleagues it is "the most certain philosophy," as one of the founding fathers of the French historical school put it.[32]

It was most certain because no other method existed; the old certainties were gone. Only theologians, presumably, were equipped to grasp the meaning of universal history in the old sense of the phrase. Was that a polite way of saying that it was a futile task, considering the proverbial ignorance of theologians? The four monarchies, the seven ages, and all the other feeble imaginings of clerics whose knowledge of Latin and history was pathetically inadequate, all this nonsense had to be cleared away together with the stock of fables such as the legend of Trojan origins. As La Popelinière wrote apropos of the latter, "When you want to construct a great building you have to sink the foundations in a clear and safe site; in the same way, if you wish to engrave a straight opinion on man's brain, you have to clear it first of errors and obscure clouds."[33]

Universal history, once an imposing construction, now lay in ruins. The old Christian guesswork about God's plan for his chosen people had become irrelevant to historians, for its truths could not be verified by historical criticism. The more respectable truths of the pagan histories could afford some glimpses of local history. The works of Thucydides and of Taci-

---

[31] La Popelinière, *Histoire des histoires,* p. 37.

[32] "Certissima philosophia," Andrea Alciato called it in his *Encomium historiae* (1518), quoted by Kelley, "Historia Integra," p. 35.

[33] La Popelinière, *Dessein,* p. 383.

tus would, of course, be admitted as evidence by future historians, but only to the extent that they reported contemporary events in a trustworthy fashion. The contribution of the classical histories to general history was small; one could not even begin to guess at the complete shape of man's past by consulting them. The exploration of this hidden shape had become a very important matter. Nothing was more important than the eventual discovery of the true nature of universal history, this perfection which some day, perhaps, would become visible, if only dimly, to the New Historian.

Only a generation earlier, universal history had meant the shape of God's plan as revealed in prophecy and interpreted by theologians; or it had meant simply the *corpus* of classical histories strung together, a narrow beam of light thrown on one portion only of the human story, all the rest to be left eternally in the dark. The first of these conceptions was now judged irrelevant, the second woefully inadequate. If there ever had been an accepted version of universal history, there was none now. One would have to start all over from scratch.

Slowly, painfully, uncertainly, the past would be reconstructed. Large portions of it would perhaps elude the historian's grasp forever, if by history one meant certainty about the past. "But where would we be," writes La Popelinière, "if we could speak only of things we know with certainty?" Historical research, he admits, begins in ignorance and uncertainty; "one advances in fear, by making conjectures, and one proceeds by suspending judgment, as it were, until at last the end appears in sight as clear and assured as the beginning was full of doubts."[34]

There was hope because the New Historian, as a result of the labors of a generation of scholars, now stood equipped with an adequate method for the critique of the surviving records. Cujas, Alciato, Budé, Hotman, Pasquier, Pithou, Du Tillet,

---

[34] La Popelinière, *Histoire des histoires,* p. 36.

Vignier, and La Popelinière, among others, had achieved at least that much. With their works to guide him, the future historian would know where to look for the raw materials with which he was to construct his "perfect history." He would know how to authenticate these records and how to select from them. Most of all, he would no longer be burdened with the impossible questions of the medieval theologians, questions which he could never have answered. He would not run the danger of sinking into the thankless task of writing particular or simple histories, if he followed La Popelinière's clearly spelled out directions, the "traditive" which led to the "modelle du vray historiographe." The scope of general history, La Popelinière advised, should be neither too small nor too large; the history of France is a fine example of an appropriate subject. This is not to say that there is no place for monographs on smaller topics; such works serve as preparatory studies for general history. Nor is a larger scope to be excluded—the history of several nations or even the history of all of them—but, given the limited means at his disposal, the historian will find this immense and fascinating subject unrewarding. It is best to steer a middle course and choose a subject large enough to be significant and small enough so that the highest standards of erudition can be applied to it.

The historian, once having chosen a suitable subject for his researches, must then set out to be philosophical as he approaches the data. The *philosoph historicus*, as Bodin calls him, will search for the causes of change in history. He will approach the documents with questions in mind such as these: why does this state grow and that other decline? What is the origin of this custom and that idea? How does civilization begin and how does it end? Just precisely what is the difference between a primitive and a civilized society?

"What are the sources, the form, the environment, the growth and the transformations of all the good and bad features of the human condition, what, for that matter, is the origin of

all the ideas about society formulated by the ancient philosophers, historians and jurists?" asks La Popelinière.[35] The ulti-
mate goal of history, in sum, is to explain man. And this
certissima philosophia assumes that what man is today—his
cities, his technology, his customs, his very ideas about right
conduct—is the result of an historical process which can be
traced back to its origins.

This is why the men of the New World are so important to
know: they are, perhaps, the missing part of the equation. If
they are truly primitive, then perhaps they are in that very condition which existed in Europe and Asia before the invention
of letters. What an opportunity! They must be studied. An inventory of their way of life must be made and this must be compared with European civilization. At last an experimental
technique exists for measuring the processes of history, and the
Sieur de la Popelinière is ready to undertake the task. Let the
Estates of Holland finance his research and he would take ship
and sail at once (see Appendix II).

---

[35] These last questions La Popelinière asks in a letter to Scaliger; see Appendix II.

The sense of history

Ninth chapter

Historical-mindedness is a homely word and not a very precise one. It is used here to avoid the ambiguities of the German word *Historismus* which, to compound the confusion, is variously translated as historism or historicism. It is not necessary to devise yet another definition of historicism.[1] The pertinent question is not so much "what is historicism?" but rather

---

[1] Kelley, "Budé," gives an able exposition of the meaning of historicism as it applies to Renaissance historical thought.

151

"how did historicism come about?" Perhaps the answer to the second question will yield the answer to the first.

The question of the origins of our sense of history is a murky one treated so far mostly by German scholars. Not murky because it has been treated badly, or by Germans, but because the question touches on too many other problems which are not yet capable of historical treatment. It is too big a question and the sources belong to one of the least known periods of European history. No wonder a scholar like Meinecke, in his book on the origins of historicism, chose to "leap from mountaintop to mountaintop," from one genius to the next, from Voltaire to Montesquieu and from Leibniz to Goethe.[2] He would have been hard put to do otherwise.

Let us return to the figures, familiar by now, of Pasquier and his world. We have seen them at work, busy with their researches. We have seen them wrestle with the problems of historical generalization. Now we turn to a more diffuse line of inquiry to ask questions about their historical-mindedness. Now we have to ask whether one can speak of genuine historical-mindedness in the sixteenth century.

Meinecke flatly denied it and most students of this question have agreed with him. On the other hand, the evidence offered so far in this book refutes the notion that historical-mindedness was an invention of the eighteenth century. In all the work of the sixteenth-century historians one encounters constantly an awareness of the difference between past and present that is the essence of historical-mindedness.

The relativity of law

This awareness, as we have seen, came in part from their study of law. The teaching of Budé, Alciato, and Cujas fitted the Roman law codes into the context of Roman history and showed that these laws had functioned in a society which was

[2] Meinecke, *Entstehung des Historismus*, p. 3.

so different from contemporary French society that the two worlds had almost nothing in common.

François Hotman stated this case very clearly in his *Antitribonian* (1567): "Consider the difference between Patricians and Plebians. In this difference alone, in this distinction of the condition and quality of persons . . . on these two qualities and differences of persons, as on two hinges, the entire state rested and revolved. . . ." And, of course, there was nothing at all like this in French society.

Not only were ancient Rome and modern France quite differently constituted societies, but even the laws of Rome as represented by Justinian's code could not be said to fit the needs of any real state. This Byzantine compilation assembled not the laws of Rome but fragments from the laws of many Romes. There was the Rome of the democracy, of which only a few remains were left, "little shavings, remnants, samples only" which bore only a tenuous relationship to the whole body of republican law as it once was. To pretend to an understanding of republican law on the basis of these remnants, Hotman contended, was like imagining the shape of an ancient ship with a few pieces of wreckage as the sole clue. Then there were the laws of imperial Rome. Here the remnants were larger, no doubt, "but in all this there is only variety, diversity and change. For the government changed ordinarily according to the whims of the emperors . . ." and "the relics of this part of Roman law are thin and small. . . ." There was, finally, the law of Justinian's own time and this was largely represented, of course.[3]

What then was Roman law? Obviously, there was no such thing, nor could there be. For laws changed constantly, in keeping with the needs of society. Roman law as it was known through late compilations was a collection of relics.

All law was the product of history, of history and of nothing else. It was, therefore, always different and always unique, at

---

[3] François Hotman, *Antitribonian* (1567), in *Opuscules françoises des Hotman* (Paris, 1616), pp. 9–10.

all times a mirror held up to society. "Any man of good sense," Pasquier would claim, "can almost imagine what a nation was like, without reading a general history, simply by looking up its ancient statutes and ordinances; and by the same token, he can imagine what a people's laws are if he knows their way of life."[4]

There was an absolute correspondence between law and society; that much was clear to all the disciples of Cujas. But if law was the product of history, as they all believed, what place could one make for the cherished and ancient doctrine of natural law?

On receiving a treatise, *Du droit de nature*, written by a colleague, Pasquier in his reply to the author took up the issue of natural versus historical law. Are our laws founded on natural law? he asked. "Before replying," he added prudently, "let me say that I exclude all sacred laws from this discussion for fear of impiety."

Pasquier grants only one extra-historical quality to man. This one quality, inherent not only in human but in all animal nature, is an instinct for self-preservation. This instinct, Pasquier believes, is the only constant element in human behavior. On the individual level, it manifests itself among men in the form of the sex drive (here Pasquier prudently observes that the instinct is suspended by God's will in the case of those chosen to shine in saintliness). Men procreate and seek sufficient food and comfort to preserve their lives and those of their progeny. They also instinctively try to defend themselves when threatened by other men or natural calamities. On a larger level, the individual instinct for self-preservation is mirrored in the entire human community's attempts at preserving society.

This much Pasquier grants to nature. "But having taken this first step, I can go no farther," he insists. "I dare not go farther, I cannot judge whether all the other laws which result from this instinct for the preservation of society are founded on nature

4 Pasquier, *Recherches* (1607), p. 543.

or merely on opinion." His position is very clear. All laws, at all times, clearly are made for the purpose of preserving society, but this purpose was understood in different ways in different societies at various times. Furthermore, the differences are so great and each law is so uniquely the expression of a given historical situation that it is impossible to say that one law is in conformity with nature while another is not.

To safeguard society, men have usually devised some kind of political constitution. Most of these have fallen into one of three main types: royal, seigneurial, or popular governments. In each case people have thought of their own constitution as the best. How then can one system of government be demonstrated to be natural to the exclusion of all the others? (What a subversive thought—soon French publicists would get busy to show that monarchy alone was natural.) Further, the economic and social organization of society follows no set pattern either. Plato and Lycurgus approved the community of goods. Some societies practiced the common ownership of women. Others favored polygamy. Had you talked with the lawmakers of all these different societies, Pasquier suggests, each of them would have given you plenty of reasons to show that their laws were the best of all possible laws.

How far can Pasquier push this historical relativism? Will he subject the laws of his own country to it? He does not avoid the question. L'Eschacier, the author of *Du droit de nature*, held the orthodox and patriotic view that the French Salic law of royal succession was in conformity with natural law. "I readily believe that," Pasquier replies slyly, "because, like yourself, I was born under that law. But take a look at England," he continues, "and you will find the English thinking their law as natural as you think yours. And yet they are very different laws. Take the rights of succession in our fiefs—talk about these laws with the Emperor Justinian and he will tell you there is nothing so unreasonable as the inequality between male and female rights."

Pasquier draws his comparisons from Roman and Byzantine

law, from medieval customary law, from the reports of the explorers in the New World. Everywhere, he concludes, men fashion laws entirely according to their needs, although the common purpose of all law, obviously, is the preservation of society. "You will say that I am mistaken in attributing laws to opinion, not nature," he writes. "I reply that I will be glad to attribute laws to nature if you will tell me what has been our nature since Adam wanted to taste the fruit of knowledge. Since then our nature has been so depraved that it hardly merits to be called anything more than opinion." The careful wording here, the shrewd appeals to orthodox Christian sentiments do not hide the meaning—man has no nature, only a history.[5]

The mutations of language

Languages, like laws, change constantly. Their birth, growth, evolution, and decline are governed, as are all things, by the history of the societies which use them. That was one of the most frequently expressed theories of language in the erudite circles of sixteenth-century Paris.

The nature of the French language, its relationship to other languages, its degree of development, its grammar and spelling, all these were the subjects of lively controversies. Everybody in Paris had opinions on the French language and practically everybody, or so it seems, rushed into print with his opinions.[6] The most common argument was a patriotic one: Frenchmen should use their own language; an end should be put to the servile imitation of Romans or Italians. The French language is as good as any other—in fact, it is better. These rhetorical

[5] The letter quoted here can be found in Pasquier, *Oeuvres*, II, Book XIX, Letter 7, pp. 551–554.

[6] Among the principals in these controversies over the nature of the French language were Jacques Pelletier du Mans, Joachim du Bellay, Jean Bodin, Pierre de La Ramée, Abel Mathieu, Amyot, Le Roy, Henri and Robert Estienne, Charles Bouëlles, Jacques Dubois, Drosay, Meigret, Geoffroy Tory, and De Baif. See F. Brunot, *Histoire de la langue française* (Paris, 1906), vol. II.

defenses of the French language reflected some genuine problems. The use of Latin was often impractical. The French language, on the other hand, was in need of definition: grammar, spelling, and pronunciation were all in doubt.

One thing was clear, however: this was that language changed, and changed rapidly. That is why the task of the translator was so unrewarding, Pasquier pointed out. "The translator works like a slave and tortures his wits trying to follow as closely as possible the author whom he is translating, he uses up his life at this work, he hunts down all the most elegant phrases current in his time to fit them to the original language of the author. Meanwhile his native tongue changes slowly with time, it is as if we had bought a new dress for it and were ready to discard the old. This is why we abandon old translations . . . and want to go directly to the original books be they Greek or Latin. . . ."[7]

This feeling for the ephemeral nature of language was common. Here, for instance, is Montaigne on the same subject: "I write my book for a few men and a few years. If it were a question of lasting, I should have had to use a more durable language. Judging from the variations suffered by our own language up to now, who can hope that it will be used in its present form fifty years hence? It flows through our hands every day and it has been half changed in my lifetime."[8]

Montaigne's notion that his own language was more vulnerable to the ravages of time than Latin was fairly common. However, it was also clearly understood that Latin was a dead language and that it could not, without major changes in its vocabulary, serve the purposes of Frenchmen. As early as 1552 Pasquier pointed this out and argued for the adoption of French as the language of law, scholarship, and science. "The titles of our France, the military instruments, the terms of law, in short half the things we use today have changed and have nothing

---

[7] Pasquier, *Lettres* (Lyon, 1597), p. 56.

[8] Quoted in *Dictionnaire des lettres françaises* (XVIᵉ siècle), p. 10.

in common with the language of Rome. In view of this mutation it is foolish to want to express in Latin that which never
was Latin." The French language in his own time may be in-
ferior to Latin in some respects, Pasquier may be willing to
grant (in 1552). If this is so, there are reasons for it which
one ought to look for not in the inherent quality of the two
languages, but in the social conditions which created and developed them. The Latin language was developed in a democracy where public speaking was an art essential to government.
French, on the other hand, was the language of a monarchy in
which public speaking had never played an important part.
Things grow only when they are nurtured.[9]

The fundamental principle with which Pasquier and his colleagues approach the study of language is that all language is
the product of history. It cannot be regulated or regimented by
professors and it has no abstract or absolute rules: ". . . the
people are the sovereign lords of the language," wrote Pierre
de La Ramée. "The school of language is not in the lecture halls
of the professors of Hebrew, Greek and Latin at the University
of Paris . . . it is at the Louvre, in the law courts, in the mar-
kets . . ." and other popular places.[10] Or, as Pasquier summed
it up: language expresses the way of life of its users ("language
symbolize ordinairement avec nos moeurs").

As the *moeurs* of a people change, so does its language. This
natural, unconscious *mutation* "proceeds from our own minds,
just as clothes, magistrates, even governments take on different
appearances in the history of a people," wrote Pasquier,[11] and
La Popelinière thought that the modern languages in his time
were far from having reached their fullest development.[12]

[9] Pasquier, *Oeuvres*, II, p. 3.

[10] Quoted in *Dictionnaire des lettres françaises* (XVIe siècle), p. 12.

[11] Pasquier, *Oeuvres*, I, p. 751.

[12] "Car ie maintiens contre l'advis de tous ceux qui ont parlé et ecrit des
langues, qu'aucune de celles de tant de Peuples retirez de l'obeissance de
l'Empire Romain n'a encore atteint sa perfection. Voire n'est venue au point
de sa consistance." La Popelinière, *Idée*, p. 254.

The variation of faith

The historical-mindedness which operated so visibly in the case of law and language extended to all matters. It was a way of looking at the world, a method as irresistible and as universally applicable in Pasquier's generation as the mathematical method was to be a generation later. It was, as the Jesuits knew, a very dangerous method. Its application to religion is a vast and important subject all of its own. Here I can only touch on it.

Among intellectuals the Reformation was at bottom an historical question, as they kept battling each other with documents to support their notion of what the primitive church had been like and measuring the historical variations of their opponents from this standard. Among the theologians, some resisted the historical method while others adopted it eagerly. There were others still who accepted the historicizing approach of the respected *érudits* with reluctance, making their accommodation with what seemed the inevitable. This last position is very well put by the Protestant theologian Nicolas Vignier, the son of the historian, on the occasion of the posthumous publication of his father's *Church History*:

> Although the approbation of the Christian Religion should not rest on Chronology, but on Theology, not on the customs of men but on the truth of God, it happens, nevertheless, in this last of ages, that one does battle rather by the calculation of years than by the solidity of reasons. That is the source of this controversy concerning the Antiquity [of Protestantism] so often used in argument. That is the source of those voices which ask, where do you come from? Where were you? Whom did you succeed? Would God have forgotten his Church over so many centuries? Did the Gates of Hell prevail over God's Church? Could God's sacred ordinance have been violated? And, look, say others, was not the brazen serpent, the image of Christ's cross, used for criminal superstitious purposes? Was not the name of God, which surpasses all things in holiness, in fact exposed every day to the

blasphemy of men? Was not baptism, our Lord's sacred institution, abused in the very time of the Apostles—or soon after—and given to the living acting as proxy for the Dead?

Therefore one has to go back to the source and say with our Lord Jesus Christ: it was not always thus since the beginning. . . . Jesus Christ is my antiquity, said St. Ignatius, and not to obey him is manifest perdition. My authentic archives are his cross, his death, his resurrection. . . . That which comes first is the most true, said Tertullian. That which is at the beginning is first: that which is of the Apostles is at the beginning.

It is therefore a very necessary thing to know what doctrines were held from that very beginning in the Church and to see graphically represented the various mutations experienced by the Church; how sickness succeeded health and error truth; by what writers, by what means, with what progress, and at what times the Church was glorious and at what times it fled to the desert. And that is the content of this book.[13]

The historicist mentality of the Parisian intellectuals of this generation was reducing religion itself to a custom among men. Politics and law, language and religion, all these were expressions of the *moeurs* of a particular society. These *moeurs* and their *mutation* were the proper subjects of the historians' interest. The historical method was applicable to all things human: the Roman church, the religion of the Brazilians, or the history of tennis could all be studied in the same way. In his *Recherches* Pasquier makes this point very emphatically by simply refusing to arrange his essays in a strict topical order. Here one can find the history of children's games next to the history of the *parlement*, and, quite seriously, the history of the game of tennis in Book IV among other essays on social history.[14] Even in such

[13] Nicolas Vignier, *Recueil de l'histoire de l'Eglise* (Leyden, 1601). The passage quoted is from the younger Vignier's dedication to the Marquis de Rosny, written in 1599. (That is the date of the *privilège*.)

[14] Pasquier, *Oeuvres*, I, p. 395. Among other essays on social history in this part of the *Recherches*, there are essays on criminal procedure; social classes (*de l'Estat & condition de personnes de nostre France*); on the history of customs relating to the treatment of prisoners of war; on the history of

small things, historical research appears to bear out Pasquier's philosophy. The rules of tennis are no exception to the general *mutation* of *moeurs*: like all else, they grow from small beginnings and in time, stimulated by rewards, they gravitate toward what works best.

Historical relativism

The highest expression of historicism is to consider historiography itself subject to the *mutations* of time. To say that the historian's method—the instrument which allows us to measure the difference between old and new, between French and Roman—is itself only the expression of a given society's customs at some time and that it, too, changes in keeping with the general *mutation* of the human community is to cast profound doubts on the findings which led to this conclusion in the first place. It is always difficult to accept such a position and it was especially difficult to defend it in the sixteenth century in the face of the attacks "against history." On the other hand, it was so natural a position to take, it was so much the reasonable next step after all the other steps taken, that it must have been just as difficult to resist. The critical reading of old laws led to the discovery that all law was the product of history. The

---

notaries, curfews, gypsies, real estate laws, artillery, printing, and chess. Pasquier, who was addicted to the game of tennis, could not resist looking into its history. Why was it called the palm-game (*jeu de paulme*), he wondered, since it was played with a racket and not with the palm of one's hand. He discovered, by consulting an old manuscript, which he quotes and which describes the feats performed in 1427, by a 28-year-old female champion named Margot, that tennis at that time was played without rackets. Not content with a single source, our historian controls it with the oral testimony of an old champion named Gastelier whom he used to know in his youth. Gastelier, Pasquier tells us, was at least seventy-six years old at that time, but he used to hang around the tennis courts and talk about the old days. It seems that in Gastelier's time the game was played with bare hands, but sometime later the players took to wearing thick leather gloves for protection; further refinements, such as strings strung across the gloved palms for more power, led in time to the introduction of regular rackets.

critical reading of old histories should have led to a similar conclusion: all histories were also the product of history.

The implications of this idea were so unsettling—they played straight into the hands of the Pyrrhonists—that few could take this final step and only a wild theorist like La Popelinière, writing at a time when he had perhaps less than ever to lose, would go so far as to write an entire book in support of this notion. That is what the *Histoire des histoires* is. Dense, confusing, and full of verbiage and histrionic poses as it is, the book nevertheless has a consistent thesis; it is not merely a catalogue of names. La Popelinière may need an interpreter, and it is true that he often does not know his own mind. But this is not surprising, considering the difficulty of what he was trying to say and the circumstances in which he was writing.[15]

He undertakes to write the history of histories in order to show how the discipline evolved from its distant origin in folk memory to its present state. He tries to show that this development followed the same pattern everywhere in the world and that each society had a historiography suitable to its own stage of evolution on the long path from savagery to civilization. The songs and dances observed among the Indians of the New World and in Africa are comparable to those of the ancient

[15] He had spent his patrimony on books and the other necessities of his profession. The publication of his own books could not have brought in much money, especially since they were shamelessly plagiarized. Only a few years after the publication of the *Histoire des histoires* in January, 1604, the old historian, disappointed, almost certainly hungry and cold, wrote a letter to Scaliger in which he proposed that the Dutch government should underwrite an expedition he proposed to lead to unexplored territories. He hasn't too much hope, he admits, but the old flame is still there. He wants a research grant and he is surely starving, but he still gets excited about his project, which is to be a scientific study of primitive societies on a universal scale. He wants to find out "what difference there is between savage and civilized peoples," and to "find out just how men (starting out from a condition which is said to have been savagery and isolation) have gradually made themselves social and united by the various bonds of human institutions." See Appendix II. La Popelinière's letter, of course, produced no results. Not long afterwards he died, in the heart of winter, sitting in front of a fireplace, of a malady, it was rumored, common to men of letters: hunger.

Hebrews he had read about in Josephus' history, or to Homer's songs, or to those of the primitive Germans, Gauls, and Britons noted by Tacitus and Caesar. "Such was the earliest memory, that is to say the earliest history, of all peoples, including the most barbaric."[16]

City life and the use of writing gradually transformed the primitive tribal memory into the kind of history practiced by the Greeks and of which Herodotus' history was the earliest example. Civilized history, no less than primitive history, reflected the conditions of the society in which the historian lived. This has been its most serious shortcoming. The Roman historians, for instance, wrote from the narrow Roman point of view of the upper classes. Roman culture was class-bound, presumably because of the Roman fear of their slaves.[17] This social rigidity inhibited historiography, which flourishes only in an atmosphere of liberty. Under the autocratic rule of the emperors, things went from bad to worse, when ". . . the state became subject to the domination of a single man . . ." and historiography consequently ". . . became the slave to the passions of the rulers."[18]

Medieval historiography suffered from the same disease. It, too, was class-bound. The historians were clerics and saw all things from the point of view of the church. The early chroniclers ". . . can talk only of miracles, predictions, dreams, apparitions and other such extraordinary things, knowing no busi-

[16] La Popelinière, *Histoire des histoires*, p. 28.

[17] "Encor qu'on puisse attribuer le motif de cette deffense à la crainte que ces sages politics avoyent que plus de 3 ou 400 mil esclaves ne se reconussent à Rome, entre 50 ou 60 mil citoyens, par une determinée fricassée desquels ils peussent en un jour renverser tout l'estat des Romains. . . ." La Popelinière, *Idée,* p. 234.

[18] On the relationship between historiography and liberty: "Doncques le deffaut des Histoires tant Romaines que autres, ne doit estre rapporté à la seule perte de la fleur des langues, tant qu'au declin des bonnes moeurs et de la liberté surtout"; on the influence of autocracy: "A l'occasion de quoy l'histoire fust aussitost alterée de sa premiere pureté. Et ainsi que l'estat estoit asservy à la domination d'un seul, aussi l'histoire fut rendue serve des passions de ceux qui commandoient." *Ibid.,* p. 235.

ness except that of the Church: in all other matters they are mere chroniclers." He means here that the medieval church-men could be considered as historians only in the field of church history. They did not know enough about other things to be of use except as chroniclers—purveyors of unevaluated, raw information. This was not without its advantages, as he realized, because they were too naïve to lie: "They at least seem to work in good faith and conscientiously."[19]

The later medieval historians did not even possess this saving grace. They were hacks in search of honor or profit. War was the only subject which interested them, and even on this subject they knew no better than to trust hearsay and rumor. They were idle, full of book learning, and shut away from the affairs of this world. Their understanding was limited to the "the form of accidents" and mundane appearances.[20] That is, they spent too much time describing the dress of the participants and the heralds' speeches, as in the example of Monstrelet.

"Historiography steers a course which follows the fluctuations of states as closely as a ship follows the movement of the mariner's compass."[21] In the broadest sense this is inescapable. Nationalism always imposes a bias from which historians have never completely escaped. Among all the historians he has read, La Popelinière never found one "who could shed his love of his own country or his hatred of its enemies."[22] Religious bias, again in the broadest sense, was just as inescapable; one simply should not trust a Jewish historian when he writes about Christians, nor should one trust a Christian historian writing about Jews.[23] There never was a historian who could free himself either from his own particular prejudices or from those imposed

---

[19] La Popelinière, *Dessein*, p. 345.

[20] *Loc. cit.*

[21] "L'histoire se regle au compas du gouvernement de l'Estat." La Popelinière, *Histoire des histoires*, p. 374.

[22] La Popelinière, *Idée*, p. 216.

[23] La Popelinière, *Dessein*, p. 321.

on him by others to the point where he could report everything he knew truthfully.[24]

With history itself stripped of every kind of absolute authority by his historicizing compulsion, one might think that La
Popelinière would succumb to the arguments of the Pyrrhonists,
who demanded to know, "What certainty can be have concerning events of long ago, since we are unsure and without
agreement about events which happen in our own time and
in front of our own eyes?"[25]

This disturbing argument was not new. Like Vignier and
the other experimental historians of his generation, La Popelinière had thought about this difficulty many times. The same
historical-mindedness which forced him to recognize the limitations of historical research also enabled him to make his peace
with a discipline which was less than definitive in its results.
"One must judge an historian's achievement like that of archers
shooting in competition: the best is the one who hits the target
most frequently and misses it least often,"[26] he admitted. Perfect history was impossible, he concluded reluctantly.[27] But,
such as it was, the historical method still represented the most
certain philosophy in an uncertain world.

Despite his qualms and doubts, despite the past record of
historians, he believed in the possibility of a more scientific
history. The New History he was advocating would inevitably
have its shortcomings. The historians could never hope to be
completely emancipated from the pressures of their environment, but an awareness of these pressures and a determined
resistance to them would raise the science to a level never yet

[24] La Popelinière, *Ideé,* pp. 216–217.

[25] Charles de La Ruelle, *Succintz adversaires contre l'histoire et professeurs
d'icelle* (Poitiers, 1574), p. 16. La Ruelle goes on to give an example: "The
death of the late Sieur of St. André, marshal of France—killed in battle in
full sight of the entire camp—which was reported by a hundred men in a
hundred different versions, each claiming to know the truth of it. . . ."

[26] La Popelinière, *Idée,* p. 7.

[27] *Ibid.,* p. 35.

attained. The New Historian must refuse patronage of any kind; he must be in debt to neither state nor church.[28] He must keep his eyes steadily fixed on posterity and try to avoid the passions of his own day. These prophylactic measures, together with a sound critical method and free access to the documents, would result in as good a history as was humanly possible—and no one could ask for more.

Here then is historical-mindedness—historicism, if you will —solidly established in the mental habits of a handful of scholars in the sixteenth century. Neither Locke's psychology nor the scientific revolution seem to have been prerequisites for the growth of a sense of history as we understand it. This state of mind existed in all its essentials before 1600. It disappeared again—or at least it was weakened and suppressed—in the course of the next century, precisely during the time when science and Cartesian rationalism became important features of European culture.

It might be objected that the historical-mindedness of a few avant-garde intellectuals can be written off as a kind of historical oddity. They were precursors, one might say, men "ahead of their time," as Vico, for instance, was ahead of his time with his *Scienza nuova*. Such accidents happen and have only a small place in the study of a large problem like that of the origins of historicism.

However, the notion of "men ahead of their time" is an unhistorical one. Vico, as a matter of fact, far from being ahead of his time (in Naples, of all places, a backwater, isolated from most contemporary currents of thought), was a distant disciple of the sixteenth-century jurists and historians, a straggler in the history of ideas, echoing Bodin, not announcing Hegel.[29]

[28] "C'est en somme un pas fort glissant qu'une liberale magnificence envers l'Historien." La Popelinière, *Dessein*, p. 370.

[29] See Franco Simone, "Introduzione ad une storia della storiografia letteraria francese," *Studi francesi* 8 (1964), p. 445; Simone, "La coscienza storica del Rinascimento francese e il suo significato culturale," *Convivium* 22 (1954),

The philosophical historians of the nineteenth century, Michelet in particular, discovered Vico and saw a precursor in him, a like-minded historicist isolated in the century of the Enlightenment. They did not go back far enough beyond Vico to the sources of his philosophy.

It would be useful to know just how much influence the sixteenth-century historical movement did exert in its own time. I think that one can safely assert that the ideas of Bodin, Pasquier, Le Roy, Vignier, or La Popelinière reached a very large part of the educated reading public of their generation in France. The success of the erudite historians reflected a general interest in history among educated Frenchmen; indeed, it appeared to some as a veritable craze. In 1574 La Ruelle was of the opinion that "Frenchmen think so highly of history and employ so great a part of their time in reading it" that this vogue might turn out to be harmful to the nation. The popularity of history in this period is a strong impression that one cannot avoid. The recent statistical study made by Corrado Vivanti measures this vogue and confirms the general impression. Vivanti counts 657 history books published in France between 1550 and 1610. Of these 271 are first editions and 386 are reimpressions. More than half of this publishing activity is concentrated in the years 1560–1588. After this high point, there is a decline. Vivanti also observes a shift occuring within this general movement. He notes that the old chronicles are re-edited less frequently as time goes on, while the new kind of historical work, the institutional histories modeled on Pasquier's *Recherches*, grow in popularity.[30]

The extraordinary demand for historical works, especially of the new kind, in the late sixteenth century—extraordinary by comparison with the previous half century and probably

pp. 156–170; A. D. Momigliano, "Vico's Scienza Nuova," *History and Theory* 5 (1966), pp. 3–23; also Frank E. Manuel, *Shapes of Philosophical History* (Stanford, Calif., 1965), Chap. 3.

[30] Corrado Vivanti, "Paulus Aemilius Gallis condidit historias?" *Annales: Economies, sociétés, civilisations* 19 (1964), pp. 1117–24.

also by comparison with the next half century—is one measure of the general popularity of history and, indirectly, also a measure of the temporary triumph of the new historicism.

This is not to say that the historical philosophy of La Popelinière, for example, was widely accepted or even understood, any more than Collingwood's philosophy or Febvre's ideas are in our own time. This kind of influence is not to be expected. Nonetheless, one can see that at least some parts of this philosophy in diluted form had a wide enough attraction to be incorporated in the works of more traditional and more popular writers. We see such an example in Belleforest's history.

Historians like Pasquier or Vignier did not write in a vacuum; their outlook was largely the product of the kind of education they had received, an education which was common to a large segment of the *robin* class. There was in sixteenth-century France a clear and generally accepted idea of what a good education should be. While it is true that the culture of the age was largely created by and for the learned and wealthy magisterial class (see Appendix I), it is also true that the humanist curriculum of the *collèges* was not merely a preparation for law school. The humanist magistrates were, in principle, prescribing an education intended as a *magistra vitae* for men of all classes. So it is that one can find entirely poor men of no social standing like Le Roy as well as kings appreciating the classical culture dispensed in Paris by the royal professors.[31] The historical thought naturally expressed by classically edu-

---

[31] The royal professors or *lecteurs* began teaching in 1530, and within three years no distinguished young man with anything like a reputable secondary education behind him would consider attending courses at the Sorbonne. See A. Lefranc, *Histoire du Collège de France* (Paris, 1893), p. 138. The famous (and ill-paid) scholars and scientists who formed the corporation of the king's professors, later to become the Collège de France, lectured to large audiences. They also had teaching assistants. In addition, a kind of free university functioned side by side with the official teaching and complemented it. Furthermore, it was customary for the students to live in at intellectual *pensions,* such as the one run by Sturm, where their monthly dues paid for room and board, but also for conversation, tutoring, informal seminars, and library privileges.

cated lawyers like Pasquier found a wide audience because French culture in his time was a *culture de robe*. It may be that the New History became less attractive to later generations because the political and intellectual predilections of the *robins* ceased to exercise their once dominant influence; education was increasingly in the hands of Jesuits and Oratorians; Italian and Spanish intellectual fashions dominated at court; and within French society the *robins* had lost much of their power and self-confidence. In this new world the monarch was not only hostile to the *robins* but badly educated as well and quite incapable of understanding the ideas of the *doctes, curieux*, and *sçavans* who had delighted his ancestors.[32]

---

[32] In 1670 Molière's *Cleonte* is unwilling to call himself a *gentilhomme* although he comes of a *robin* family and he himself served in the military for several years. Compare this diffidence with the characteristic behavior of the same kind of man a century earlier (see Appendix I).

Conclusions

Tenth chapter

What happened to the New History after 1600? Pasquier studied the records of the trials of Joan of Arc, but he had no successors (see Appendix III); the origins of the French were explained in the most authoritative fashion only to become an open question again; the providential theory of universal history was discarded only to be resurrected by Bossuet and his contemporaries; the idea of natural law was exposed to an historicist attack, but natural law survived and historicism had to be reinvented in the nineteenth century. It would appear

170

that the sixteenth-century historical movement had no successors.[1] La Popelinière, who in 1572 had full confidence in the ability of his contemporaries to produce the New History he dreamed of, had already given up his dream in 1599, when he no longer expected to see his ideal achieved in his lifetime. If anything, he contended, the French were now "working against the grain" of his ideas.[2] And in many ways he seems to have been right. His own *Idea of History* was never reprinted and if his name survives at all, it is because of his history of the civil wars. His attempts to prove that the historian could be more than a witness, more than a recorder and memorialist—these proved futile.

The French climate of opinion in the seventeenth century did not prove to be receptive, on the whole, to the New History. Under Louis XIII and Louis XIV new generations in the history of French civilization were coming of age, new generations whose tastes, opinions, and secret fears were quite different from those of the age of Henri III and Henri IV.[3] A new *siècle*

[1] That was the conclusion of Gabriel Monod in his essay, "Du progrès des études historiques en France depuis le XVIe siècle," *Revue historique* 1 (1876), pp. 5–38.

[2] La Popelinière, *La vraye et entiere histoire* (La Rochelle, 1573), Preface; and *Dessein*, p. 333.

[3] See a similar point of view in Lucien Febvre's suggestive essay on the archives of Amiens, "Changement de climat: A Amiens: de la Renaissance à la Contre-Réforme," in *Au coeur religieux du XVIe siècle* (Paris, 1957). Febvre observed the new interest in history after 1560, in the books and pictures owned by the bourgeois whose possessions are catalogued in their wills. Two inventories of 1617 serve as a quick sketch of the two types of mentality, the two civilizations, which confront each other under Louis XIII. The first, represented by Pierre de Famechon's library, contains the works of Erasmus and Rabelais and the *politique* satires of the 1570s and 1580s. Here, also, can be found the *parlementaire* literature against the Jesuits; histories of the Indies, America, and Florida; Simmler's *Swiss Republic* in French translation; and Sleidan, Martin du Bellay's *Mémoires*, and other works on the civil wars. The other library, that of Martin de Miraulmont, who died the same year, is the very opposite of the first: the works of the Jesuits, of the Spanish mystics, of the Ligueurs; the *Oeuvres spirituelles* of Father Louis of Granada, the *Summa benedicti*, the *Lives of Saints*, and the *Amiens Breviary*. As Febvre concludes: "Here we are then, two kinds of men:

was at hand: the *grand siècle*, whose leaders were moved by an hysterical fear of the preceding age. In the realm of politics this fear manifested itself in an exaggerated worship of royal absolutism, which was a way of exorcising the haunting past of the civil wars. The drive for religious conformity had similar motives. It was a passionate conformity they sought, the saints and bishops of the seventeenth century and their supporting troops—that army of teachers, confessors, and courtiers who wielded the weapons of orthodoxy in boys' schools, in private chambers, and at court.

The defenders of orthodoxy quite rightly saw a more serious threat in the libertinism of intellectuals than in religious sectarianism.[4] State and church were well equipped to fight hostile sects. But the adherents of history, like the worshippers of science, showed signs of wanting to rise above sects and of assuming a frightening, unanswerable new authority. It was not a question of pitting one opinion against another; the best elements of the European intellectual community saw in Valla's critique of the Donation of Constantine as absolute a proof as in Galileo's observations. Neither case was a matter of opinion. History, it was claimed, rested, like astronomy, on "ocular demonstrations." Against these there was no defense except the refusal to look.

Historical criticism as it had been practiced by the sixteenth-century scholars became equated with libertinism. A good example of this point of view is a book entitled *Les recherches des Recherches et autres oeuvres de Me. Estienne Pasquier.* This shrill attack against Pasquier was published anonymously in 1622 by the Jesuit Father Garasse. It is a very tedious book, but it reveals the worst fears of the new conformists. While Garasse condemns Pasquier as a libertine, he does more than

the divided France of the time of Louis XIII. Which of the two kinds will prevail? That is the question. I mean, if Louis XIV is to establish himself, temporarily, on the ruins of the past."

[4] See René Pintard, *Le libertinage érudit dans la première moitié du XVIIe siècle,* 2 vols. (Paris, 1943).

that: he condemns the historical method itself. His indignation is undoubtedly genuine. What is it that bothers him so much about Pasquier and his method? "That a subject should dare to think, to say, to write that his King was *silly, or given to being silly,* that is an outrage and an intellectual aberration which ought to be punished," writes Garasse.[5] (This is apropos of a casual comment of Pasquier's on Louis XI.) "Who will believe a hundred years hence that Pasquier was a Frenchman?" exclaims the patriotic Jesuit.[6] Elsewhere Pasquier had suggested that Clovis became a convert to Christianity because, among other reasons, it was politically expedient: this is *lèse-majesté* in Garasse's eyes.[7] Then there is Pasquier's attitude toward authorities. This is an impertinence which drives Garasse to a paroxysm of fury: "When you are telling some important story taken from Moses or Xenophon or Caesar, or Thucydides or Paolo Emilio, an *impertinent* will tell you coolly: this is false, you are mistaken, it is not as you say . . ."—and refer you to some ridiculous manuscript or other. "An *impertinent,* when you tell him that you read such and such a thing in Pliny, will stop you short and say: have you been there? I have. I can speak of it as an eyewitness, it is a very beautiful city."[8]

Obviously, poor Garasse speaks from personal experience. He must have met such *impertinents* in person, and he had not enjoyed those encounters. Pasquier is a monster of *impertinence*

---

[5] "Mais qu'un sujet prenne la hardiesse de penser, de dire, d'escrire que son Roy fut *un sot, ou sujet a des sottises,* c'est une outrecuidance & un desvoyement de plume, qui meriteroit chastiment." Garasse, *Recherches,* p. 79.

[6] *Ibid.,* p. 85.

[7] *Ibid.,* p. 51.

[8] "Quand vous raconterez quelque histoire d'importance prise de Moyse, de Xenophon, de Caesar, de Thucydide, de Paul Emile, un impertinent vous dira froidement, *cela est faux, vous vous trompez, il n'est pas ainsi que vous le dites, mon papier-journal & Clopinel disent le contraire.* Un impertinent, lors que vous direz que vous avez veu telle chose dans Pline, vous arrestera tout court, disant: Y avez vous esté iamais? car i'y ay esté moy; & i'en puis parler comme tesmoing oculaire, c'est une tresbelle ville." *Ibid.,* p. 184.

as Garasse sees him, because of his constant questioning of authorities. Garasse is bothered by Pasquier's frequent references to manuscripts and other original sources and he sees a connection between the old master's historical impertinences and his philosophy of life: in short, Pasquier was a libertine.

What is a libertine? Garasse is good on this subject. "By the word libertine," he explains, "I do not mean a Huguenot or an Atheist, neither Catholic nor Heretic nor yet a Politique, but rather a composite of all these qualities. . . ." He defines the libertine by giving a catalogue of libertine opinions among which he lists the view that one should be gentle toward heretics, that to punish Huguenots is barbarous, and that the Inquisition is a cruelty worthy of cannibals. On his deathbed, the libertine will have Plato's *Phaedo* read to him.[9]

A further mark of the libertine is his aloofness from all sects. Pasquier, for instance, has the audacity to write that "God has fooled the Catholics as well as the Huguenots." This is a very libertine proposition, comments Garasse. In the same spirit, Pasquier had written that the Huguenots and Papists together "have caused the entire desolation of the Kingdom."[10] To have such an opinion, Garasse points out triumphantly, to say that Papists and Huguenots both acted criminally, means that you are neither: you are a libertine.

It was quite true, of course, that Pasquier and many *robins* of his generation were neither Huguenots nor Papists; they were Gallicans. In their time the Gallican position, which cherished the independence of the French national church, had been respectable, backed by the monarchy and by a long tradition expertly expounded by generations of jurists. But in the course of the seventeenth century, the Gallican position lost much of its respectability and official support at the same time that the *robin* class as a whole was losing much of its political power. When Pasquier was a young man, the newly founded

[9] *Ibid.,* p. 681.
[10] *Ibid.,* p. 690.

Jesuit order was accused of subversion and hounded by the powerful *parlements* and universities. By the time of his death, the Jesuits were hounding him. These changes in the fortunes of the French magistracy and in the official position toward the Gallican ideal may explain a good deal about the new crop of posthumous libertines.

One should not exaggerate the fading of sixteenth-century culture and the influence of its critics in the *grand siècle*. If Pasquier was attacked in print after his death and if his name was kept out of some standard reference works, his *Recherches*, nevertheless, went through several editions and were reprinted as late as 1723.[11] Bodin's works were ignored by the fashionable writers on politics, but, as Pierre Mesnard reminds us, Bodin continued to have a following among "those Frenchmen whom modern historical scholarship confuses too often with the mass of libertines, men who knew how to retain the use of a critical spirit in political and religious matters right in the heart of the seventeenth century. Mainly *gens de robe*, more or less keeping up the traditions of the Parisian law courts . . . royalists, but without servility, Christians, but with the greatest freedom of thought and even expression, men like Guy Patin or Ménage." Mesnard stresses the importance of this unobtrusive crowd of *sçavans* who relayed Bodin's thought to Bayle, who in turn transmitted this erudite tradition to the eighteenth century.[12]

Through the seventeenth century serious scholars in France never lost touch with the erudition of the earlier age. For one thing, scholarship in this age was often a cooperative enterprise continued over several generations. Nicolas Vignier's *Histoire de la maison de Luxembourg*, for instance, was published by André Du Chesne (1584–1640) in 1617. Du Chesne

11 In 1607, 1621, 1633, 1643, 1665, and again in 1723. At the same time, as Bouteiller points out, Pasquier's name is missing from Nicéron's *Mémoires pour servir à l'histoire des hommes illustres dans la République des Lettres.*

12 Mesnard, "Vers un portrait de Jean Bodin," in *Oeuvres philosophiques de Jean Bodin,* pp. vii–viii.

also published Pasquier's *Letters* in 1619. His own ambitious collection of medieval sources, the *Historiae Francorum scriptores*, was the realization of a project begun by Pierre Pithou (*Annalium & historiae Francorum . . . scriptores*, 1588). Du Chesne could not finish the project either; the last volumes were edited and published by his son François in the 1640s. Finally, Du Chesne's lives of the saints were published after his death by the Bollandists and the Benedictines. There, then, is a case, one among many, where the erudite tradition begun by the sixteenth-century *robins* led without interruption to the scholarly activities of religious orders in the late seventeenth century.[13]

Another striking example is that of the Godefroy family. Denis Godefroy (1549–1622) was a Protestant Parisian *robin* who taught jurisprudence in Geneva. His scholarly activities were carried on by his sons. Jacques (1587–1652) remained a Protestant, taught law in Geneva, and, like his father, published learned treatises on legal subjects. His brother Theodore (1580–1649) came to Paris and abjured in 1602—and then embarked on a long and successful career as a scholar. He was *avocat* at the *parlement* of Paris and from 1632 was royal his-

---

[13] Aside from the *Historiae Francorum scriptores* and the above mentioned editions of sixteenth-century authors, Du Chesne also published the extremely popular *Antiquitez et recherches de la grandeur et majesté des roys de France* (1609, 1614, 1624, 1629, 1631, 1637, 1648, 1668); *Bibliothèque des autheurs qui ont escript l'histoire et topographie de la France* (1618, 1627); *Histoire des papes* (1616, 1645, 1653); and *Histoire generale d'Angleterre, d'Ecosse et d'Irlande* (1614, 1634, 1641). His son François edited the posthumous editions of Du Chesne's works and wrote *Dessein de l'histoire de tous les cardinaux français de naissance* (1653, 1660) and *Histoire des chanceliers et gardes des sceaux de France* (1680). Meanwhile, Vignier's grandson Jerome, who was an accomplished antiquarian (and forger), made a career in the Order of the Oratorians, as reasonable a choice for a scholar of *robin* background in his time as the *parlement* had been in his grandfather's time. Jerome Vignier's papers were published by his friend Luc d'Achery, the founder of Benedictine scholarship and the patron of Mabillon: another glimpse of the route scholarship took from the halls of the Palace of Justice to the cloister of St. Germain des Près. See J. Havet, "Les découvertes de J. Vignier," *Bibliothèque de l'école des chartes* (1885), pp. 205–271.

toriographer. He published, notably, a collection of fifteenth-century sources for French history. His own son, Denis (1615–1681), continued Theodore's work.

Quite apart from family tradition, the professional tradition of the magisterial class continued the scholarship of the earlier generations. This is clear from even a casual reading of such directories of *sçavans* as the one provided in Jacob Spon's *Recherche* or in the pages of the *Journal des sçavans*.[14] When more becomes known about the world of scholarship in this period, I suspect that the learned Benedictine hagiographers will be seen as part of a much larger movement and the continuity of the French humanist tradition will become much more evident. The success of the reformed religious orders in attracting talented men in this period has perhaps obscured the *robin* family origin of many erudite churchmen. Bishop Bossuet himself came from a *robin* family. Jerome Vignier, a famous scholar in his time, was an Oratorian—but he was also Nicolas Vignier's grandson. The historian Le Nain de Tillemont (1637–1698) took orders in 1660 and was offered a parish in 1682, but he turned it down and lived in seclusion almost all his life, surrounded by his books. He, too, was a *robin*.[15]

One thing is absolutely clear; the sixteenth-century jurists, philologists, and historians continued to be read and continued to inspire immense respect among serious scholars, despite such attacks as Garasse's and despite the obsequious obscurantism of men like Taraut and Charron. No authority was greater among seventeenth-century scholars that that of the great *érudits* of the previous age. "I could give you an infinity of examples," runs a typical statement, "but I will

---

[14] Jacob Spon, *Recherche des antiquités et curiosités de la ville de Lyon* (Lyon, 1675), includes a directory of the *curieux de Lyon,* another of the *curieux de Paris,* and finally of the *curieux d'Europe*—which includes listings for Upsala. The *Journal des sçavans* was published from 1665 on.

[15] On Le Nain de Tillemont there is a new monograph by Bruno Neveu, which I have not had an opportunity to study.

simply tell you what Casaubon said on this subject. This author
has such a reputation among scholars that his authority is very
great for me. . . ."[16] That Casaubon was a Protestant did not
bother respectable *robins* in 1685 any more than it had a century earlier. Casaubon, Scaliger, the Estiennes, Cujas, Pasquier,
Pithou, and Bodin—most of the famous names of sixteenth-
century scholarship were tainted with heresy or libertinism.
This did not prevent them from serving as the cherished men-
tors of several generations of *érudits*.

Precise studies of the transmission of the techniques of
erudition from the time of Pasquier to the time of Bayle will
someday make it possible to speak with much greater assurance
of the history of historical scholarship. But it is already clear
that there is no break here at all. And yet there is an enormous
difference between Pasquier and Mabillon; a world separates
Bayle from La Popelinière.

The techniques of the New History were never lost; on the
contrary, they were refined and they provided the foundation
upon which modern historical scholarship was built. However,
the philosophy, the aims, and the perspectives of the sixteenth-
century movement appear to have found no direct continuation.

The *sçavans* of the seventeenth century seem to turn away
from large questions of general history. They compile glossa-
ries, like the great *robin* Du Cange (1610–1688). They write
saints' lives, like Mabillon. They edit sources for medieval
history, like Baluze (1630–1718). They study coins, like Vail-
lant (1632–1706). They tend to be antiquarians rather than
historians.

In Bodin's and La Popelinière's theoretical works, in Le
Roy's essays, in Vignier's encyclopaedia, in Pasquier's *Recherches*—in all these history had been rescued from rhetoric and

---

[16] Baudelot de Dairval (*avocat au parlement*), *De l'utilité des voyages et de
l'avantage que la recherche des antiquitez procure aux sçavans*, 2 vols.
(Paris, 1685), I, p. 37.

allied with erudition. It is this union which provoked the wrath of the libertine-hunters, it is this union which made historiography dangerous.[17] But historiography became harmless once again by divorcing itself from erudition, and erudition in turn became less dangerous as a result of this divorce.[18] The description of coins, antiquities, charters, inscriptions, and capitularies became the chief aim of historical erudition. Even the most dangerous ventures of erudition, such as Bayle's *Dictionary*, stopped short of being histories.

To the reader familiar with La Popelinière's and Vignier's insistence on history as research rather than literature,[19] and with the method of Pasquier which relies on a wide range of documentary evidence, Bayle's views, a hundred years later, will provide an astonishing contrast. For Bayle, who is a first-rate *érudit*, does not quite think of himself as an historian. History for him is a traditional literary genre which has little to do with erudition. The only time he tried his hand at history-

[17] William J. Bouwsma points out that the repression of historiography was a deliberate policy of the Counter Reformation: "Expurgation and suppression were also accompanied by an effort to make history 'safe' through its diversion from research into rhetoric and through the revival of the Ciceronian cliché *historia magistra vitae*, which reduced history to ethics teaching by example." "Three Types of Historiography in Post-Renaissance Italy," *History and Theory* 4 (1965), p. 306.

[18] The growing separation between erudition and historiography in the seventeenth century is a point made by Paul Hazard, *La crise de la conscience européenne (1680–1715)*, 3 vols. (Paris, 1935), I, p. 66, and documentation in the volume of *Notes et references*, III, pp. 36–37.

[19] "S'il est necessaire (comme plusieurs ont estimé) à celuy qui entreprend d'escrire l'estat, les faicts et gestes de quelque brave nation . . . d'avoir la cognoissance . . . des bonnes lettres avec l'ornement de la langue," remarks Vignier wryly, "ie ne doute point qu'il ne me soit imputé à temerité et outrecuidance d'avoir seulement osé toucher à l'histoire de notre France: à moy, di-ie . . . qui n'ay la grace de bien dire. . . ." Vignier, *Sommaire*, Preface. Vignier presents himself as the straight-forward technician of truth, as opposed to the flamboyant fiction-mongers like Paolo Emilio. La Popelinière, writing twenty years later, makes a positive virtue of his truly graceless style: ". . . i'ay tasché de me conformer à ceux," he explains, "qui plus soigneux de bien faire, sans parader leurs discours que de contraire: ne cherchent tant la ferveur d'une eloquence empruntée que de la verité, recommandée sur tous artifices mondains." *Histoire des histoires*, p. 3.

writing, in a life of Gustavus Adolphus which he never finished, Bayle abandoned his habit of citing sources, his style became pompous and impersonal, and above all, he limited himself to official and deliberate sources such as annals, chronicles, memoirs, and the texts of edicts and treaties: a limitation he never imposed on himself in his *Dictionary*.[20]

The fragile alliance between the practice of erudition and the writing of general history was destroyed, perhaps, in the course of the seventeenth century. Just how this happened is not yet clear, but, aside from the needs of religious and political conformity already alluded to, there were other pressures which should be taken into account. The Pyrrhonist criticism of historical knowledge, already heard in the sixteenth century, became louder and more plausible as the history books composed to satisfy the heroic aspirations of the *grand siècle* entered ever more shamelessly into the realm of fiction. The dramatic and flattering historical entertainments popular at court and the heavy-handed retelling of "stories taken from Moses, or Xenophon, or Caesar, or Thucydides or Paolo Emilio" favored by schoolmasters, free now from the interfering impertinence of scholars, drew the scorn of educated men and were responsible for the growing *pyrrhonisme de l'histoire*.

Defeated at court, suspect to the rationalists and to the ideologues of the Counter Reformation, the ideals of erudite history were kept alive nonetheless by the *sçavans*.[21] Furthermore, the "philosophical history" of the eighteenth century, much of it written by *robins*, was clearly connected with the general outlook of the earlier *robins*. In its interpretation of the past of mankind, in its humanitarian, pacifist, and elitist leanings, in all these respects the history of the *philosophes* was not far removed from the history of the *sçavans gens de*

---

[20] These are the observations of Elisabeth Labrousse, *Pierre Bayle* (La Haye, 1964), pp. 29–31.

[21] A good introduction to this uncharted field is Momigliano's essay, "Ancient History and the Antiquarian."

robe.[22] Future investigations of seventeenth-century culture and society are bound to stress the continuity of the scholarly traditions linking the French Renaissance to the French Enlightenment. It is possible that the *philosophes* owed more to the traditional outlook of a French social class than to borrowings from English scientists and philosophers.

That English laws and English philosophy—and later, American laws and American philosophy—provoked enthusiasm among French intellectuals in the eighteenth century is a fact. But why there should have been such a large audience in France for precisely such ideas, at the very moment when the *grand siècle* expired in the person of its monarch, and why those French gentlemen should then proceed to orchestrate a cultural revolution of unheard-of dimensions which relegated the rest of the world to the status of provincial admirers, has not been explained. Hazard's admirable essay has only whetted our appetites.

It may be foolish to speculate on such very broad questions at this point, but it seems clear that the modern historical mentality—with all that this implies—can no longer be regarded as a belated by-product of the scientific revolution. The modern method of explaining the past was created in the sixteenth century. It fed on the achievements of humanist erudition. It was called into being by the needs of nationalism and Protestantism, both of which required a reinterpretation of the medieval past on a scale comparable only to that which followed the triumph of Christianity in the fourth century.

---

[22] To add one more example of the striking continuity of thought between the sixteenth-century French jurists and their eighteenth-century descendants, see Donald Kelley's essay on the history of the study of feudalism, "De Origine Feudorum: The Beginnings of an Historical Problem," *Speculum* 39 (1964), pp. 207–228. Kelley shows that questions about the origins and nature of feudalism, commonly assumed to have started with Montesquieu, are the subject of scholarly controversy in the sixteenth century. Montesquieu, I need hardly add, was a descendant of the sixteenth-century jurists not only in spirit but in family and profession.

Some of the features of this new interpretation had already been thought of in Petrarch's time, and, undoubtedly, the historical method perfected by the humanists owed much to medieval and ancient learning. Our own view of antiquity and our attitude toward medieval civilization, our understanding of what constitutes proof in an historical argument—much of this was implicit in the works of some Italian humanists. It was only with the coming of a new philosophy of history, however, that humanist views and humanist learning could be put to use in interpreting the past. This "new science" has been with us much longer than we had suspected. It did not suddenly appear in the eighteenth century. It evolved slowly, as part of an infinitely complicated process, out of ancient traditions of learning. It reached maturity before 1600. Its basic impulse was not a demand for liberation from the firm mold of the medieval outlook on the past. On the contrary, the clerical culture of the Middle Ages never did organize the affairs of this world into a coherent and plausible pattern. It was the chaos of the medieval world-view—the senseless *mutatio rerum* which the bishops used to contrast with the majestic certainties of sacred history —it was this wilderness of facts which prompted the efforts of modern thinkers in their campaign for a New History.

This New History is the history we know. We cannot understand Bayle, Voltaire, Gibbon, or Montesquieu—to say nothing of the horde of lesser and more erudite contemporaries in the world of learning—without viewing them as the inheritors of a tradition already centuries old. In sum, then, the French prelude to modern historiography was more than a prelude: it was a stunning first act, full of consequences.

Appendices

Appendix I: Culture and society in France, 1540–1584
Appendix II: La Popelinière's letter to Scaliger
Appendix III: Joan of Arc: the historiographical dossier

Culture and society in France, 1540-1584

Appendix I

That magistrates—lawyers, judges, and royal officers—played a large part in the cultural life of sixteenth-century France is a generally acknowledged fact. But the full significance of this fact will escape us as long as we lack precise answers to a number of questions. It is not enough to point to this or that man of letters—Montaigne, for example—and note that he was a *robin*. How many of the poets, how many of the essayists, how many of the political theorists, how many of the writers of political pamphlets were *robins*? Ten? Fifty? Two hundred?

Is it possible that the *robins* entirely dominated certain disciplines, such as classical scholarship and historiography? Is it even possible that they dominated theology, poetry, painting, or natural science—fields not obviously connected with the magistrates' professional training and duties? Would not such a monopoly of culture, created by the natural enthusiasm of a leisured and wealthy class of people, eventually stamp the imprint of the *robin* class on French civilization? If it can be maintained that in 1584 French culture was practically synonymous with *robin* culture, was this less true in 1630 or 1660?

To begin answering such questions one has to establish some elementary facts; one has to start counting magistrates and books. This is precisely what we set out to do. The starting point of our investigation is a study of La Croix du Maine's *Bibliothèque françoise*, a bibliographical and biographical dictionary published in 1584.

La Croix du Maine was a fanatical bibliophile who set out, as a young man, to make a complete catalogue of French authors. He tells us in the preface to his book that he conceived of this project sometime after he had come to study in Paris in 1569 at the age of seventeen. He worked under severe handicaps. First of all, he was not a Parisian. Having returned to his native city, Le Mans, after two years of study, he was absent from Paris until 1582. This means that he had considerable difficulty keeping up with the literary gossip of the capital. He could not even induce printers and booksellers to send him their catalogues and brochures. Nor did he have easy access to the private libraries of Paris. His basic method of acquiring information was to buy all the books he could get his hands on. He claims in his preface to have spent over 10,000 livres in this way.

Very much aware of his status as a provincial, La Croix du Maine tried to keep in touch by publishing a prospectus of his project. In this *Discours*, of which 350 copies were printed in 1579, he invited authors to send him all the information they wished him to include in his book. The results of his call for information were disappointing. Still, he doggedly kept buying books and cultivating the acquaintance of learned men. Finally, in 1582 he packed up his books and moved to Paris, where he spent some time penetrating the inner circles of the learned world, before publishing his *Bibliothèque françoise* in 1584.

The result of La Croix du Maine's labors was a formidable reference work in which 2,095 authors are listed. The editor gives the exact titles of the published works of each author and as much biographical information as he is able to find. To be sure, this listing necessarily falls far short of being complete. First of all, the editor listed only works written in the French language, leaving works written in Latin for a later volume which he was unable to complete (he was murdered). But aside from this limitation, La Croix du Maine reached for completeness. He wished to list as many authors as possible because he wanted to show "that France is so rich in learned men . . . that it takes second place to no other nation in this respect or in any other." He deliberately exercised no selectivity. He begs us to believe "that he omitted no one of whom he had heard." As a result, many worthless writers were included, he admits, but the point of his catalogue was "to name all kinds of authors, learned ones as well as the ignorant." And it is quite true, as La Croix du Maine himself suggests, that a number of authors would be known to posterity only because he listed them.

The great advantage, for our purposes, is La Croix du Maine's heroic attempt to include all the authors he could discover. Where he fell short of this aim, we shall have to supplement his information with the help of other bibliographical works and with available catalogues of printed books. But, for a beginning, the *Bibliothèque françoise* will do very nicely.

Of the entries in the *Bibliothèque,* a considerable number is made up of medieval writers, both French and Provençal; we excluded these from consideration. We limited our inquiry to those authors whose first book was published after 1540, so that the chronological scope of our study of the relationship between magistrates and culture in France is 1540 to 1584. This is not to say that it would not be useful to test the nature of this relationship in an earlier period, for example, 1490 to 1540. That men of the *robe* were already prominent in the Republic of Letters in Budé's generation is clear. We assume, however, that the magistrates' prominence in letters, arts, and sciences increased with their numbers and their wealth and power. It is also clear that La Croix du Maine is much better informed about the men of his own generation. For these reasons the period from 1540 to 1584 seems to us a better testing ground for this preliminary inquiry.

So far, then, we have established three limitations: first, the limitation of La Croix du Maine's own horizon; second, the fact that we are only counting works written in French; and third, that we concern ourselves only with the cultural life of the period 1540–1584. There are two further limitations of minor importance; we have excluded foreigners and women. This decision should not be misconstrued as evidence of xenophobia and misogyny on our part. The inclusion of these two small categories would falsify our results, because neither foreigners nor women can easily be assigned a specific social or professional status in sixteenth-century France. Foreigners cannot be said to have belonged to a French social class and women exercised no professions.

Substance

The greatest methodological difficulty we have had to face was that of identifying those authors who could legitimately be said to have made a significant contribution to the culture of the age. La Croix du Maine lists everyone who had published anything. There are quite a few authors in his *Bibliothèque* who, for example, have published nothing but an occasional poem. Pierre Le Guillard, a magistrate from Caen who published some verse in praise of red beards, is a case in point. We excluded him. There are authors whose work may have more substance but is not exactly a contribution to culture. The case in point is that of Jean Gaultier, *maistre des comptes* in Brittany, who wrote a treatise on *The Origin, Excellence, Progress and Condition of the Office of Maistres des Comptes.* To include this kind of pamphlet would be like counting a chamber of commerce prospectus or a report to stockholders. We eliminated a large number of authors on the ground that their work was not of sufficient substance. We never gave any author the benefit of the doubt. As a result we probably eliminated a number of deserving authors. But we can be sure that those whom we counted are, in every case, what we should call genuine intellectuals.

Professional manuals excluded

Our first aim was to establish that a given author was a man of some substance. Then we took our test one step further. Among the men of substance (whose books, judging from the titles and from La Croix du Maine's comments, might even be learned and influential), there was a large number who wrote and published only in the line of their professional duty. This includes physicians who wrote medical textbooks, theologians who published collections of sermons, lawyers who published legal commentaries, and teachers who published pedagogical treatises. Much of this technical literature was probably hack work. Some of it was surely very distinguished work. Without reading one's way through all the texts, it is impossible to distinguish one from the other. One cannot simply trust La Croix du Maine, who had not read all the texts himself, nor can one simply assume that the works of quality have inevitably survived and are therefore remembered in modern reference works. In this quandary we opted for a drastic choice. We excluded all authors who published only in the line of their professional duty. Obviously, this means once again that we excluded many deserving authors. But it also means once again that those who passed our test are without question bona fide intellectuals. This test was not unknown to La Croix du Maine himself; he points out, when he wants to make sure that a particular author is understood to be *docte* or *curieux* (an intellectual in current American usage), that the man in question is so *curieux* "that he reads all sorts of good books . . . in addition to books in his own field, which is law."

Complimentary entries

Having subjected our authors to all these tests, we were left with only a few hundred. And now it became necessary to subject even those happy few to two final tests. First, we had to try to compensate for La Croix du Maine's personal bias. Some of his entries are clearly complimentary entries. This is the case when he includes friends or acquaintances for whose minds he vouches, even though there is no corroborating evidence in the form of works authored by these gentlemen. The compiler is quite aware of the difficulty, as he makes clear on a number of occasions.

In a few cases the complimentary entries refer not to friends of his but to distinguished personages—cardinals, kings, chancellors. Whenever we spotted entries of this complimentary kind we naturally eliminated them. Some of them had already been eliminated by previous tests anyway. But many had survived the other tests because the complimentary entries often describe gentlemen whose works were as yet unpublished. This brings us to the last test.

Unpublished works

Could printing and publication be our sole criterion for intellectual achievement? We thought not. There is no doubt that some fine books remained unpublished for one reason or another. An author's reticence, or his untimely death, in some cases, could account for a book remaining unpublished. La Croix du Maine himself makes no distinction between authors whose books were printed and those whose books remained un-published. In some cases, therefore, we counted unpublished works as evidence of intellectual accomplishment. This was easiest to justify in cases where the books in question were published after 1584. In other cases we had to make decisions without, of course, being at all sure. Once again we did not give the authors the benefit of the doubt. If the unpublished author, for instance, also happened to be a friend or neighbor of the compiler, we usually excluded him.

Results

The result of all this unkind scrutiny was to reduce the total number of entries to 378. These are the men, known to La Croix du Maine, who without question made significant contributions to French culture between 1540 and 1584. We should make it quite clear that this is only a probe, a preliminary inquiry. How close La Croix du Maine comes to knowing all such men in that period we cannot say. We are reasonably sure that he comes closer than anyone else. Certain fields are clearly under-represented: painters, graphic artists in general, engineers, and scientists, for example, are listed by the compiler usually only when they have written a treatise of some kind about their work. Furthermore, as engineers or engravers rarely seem to have another string to their bow—such as Greek verse or political theory—they often failed our own test of writing outside of the line of professional duty. This is a serious fault in our method.

With all these limitations understood, we have in front of us a *rare troupe* of almost four hundred men whose leadership in letters, in the arts, and in the sciences is indisputable in France between 1540 and 1584. Who were these men?

We began by asking what profession such men exercised. Some of them exercised no profession at all, to be sure, and about some we could not find out enough. These men of leisure —or about whose occupation we are in the dark—are 59 in

number. Of the remaining 319, the largest single occupational
category is magistrates—office-holding lawyers, judges, *conseillers*—*robins*, in short. These are men of recent bourgeois
origin whose office testifies to a considerable amount of wealth
and whose professional training includes the study of civil law.
There are 178 of them. The second largest category is beneficed
clerics, of whom there are 46. There are 28 pedagogues of
various sorts, ranging from private tutors through *régents* of
secondary colleges to royal professors in Paris. There are 26
physicians, 12 military men, 14 craftsmen—such as printers
or apothecaries—and 16 secretaries to the king or to other
high personages.

Several of these categories are deceptive. The holding of
clerical benefices is no index to a man's social status. Some of
these theoretical clerics are gentlemen in disguise; many
of them are in fact *robins* for whom the clerical dignity is an
honor or a business venture. Among the physicians, too, there
are many who belong to the class of the *robe*—men, that is,
whose fathers held lucrative offices in the royal bureaucracy and
whose brothers were *avocats* or *conseillers* in the *parlements*.
The secretaries are very frequently provincial *robins* who have
arrived at court.

If one tries to discover the social status of our *auteurs*, one
meets a number of deliberate roadblocks set up by status-con-
scious bourgeois or lesser *robins*. La Croix du Maine himself is
a perfect example of this. His real name was François Grudé,
and his father was a good bourgeois of the *faubourg* St. Nicolas
in the city of Le Mans. But François, who had a first-rate classical education and who moved in the most fashionable *robin*
circles of his province, never used his real name (except as an
initial G. in his *Discours* of 1579). Instead he chose to call himself "La Croix"—after a bit of land his family had, probably
no more than a farm—and since this *petite terre* was in the
province of Maine, he called himself, impressively, Monsieur de
La Croix du Maine: a perfectly successful bourgeois *gentilhomme*. At a much more exalted level you find a man like An-

toine du Verdier, the compiler of a rival reference work which
was published the same year. Du Verdier's family name was
simply Verd. But he was a wealthy and important personage in
his *pays* and well known in Lyon. He was Seigneur de Vauprivas, and owned a house in Lyon and others in the country
at Monbrison and Vauprivas. He was also *controleur general
des finances* for Lyon, *conseiller du roy,* and *élu*—tax collector
for the *pays* of Forez. He, too, is a *gentilhomme*. Another kind
of *gentilhomme* is Lancelot, Sieur de La Popelinière, born plain
Henri Voisin, who was fitted out with the name of his god-
father's country estate. He went to the University of Toulouse
to study law and spent several years commanding Huguenot
troops in Poitou: a *gentilhomme*, then, not only by virtue of the
sound of his adopted name but also by virtue of his soldiering
experience. Behind most *gentilhommes* lurks a similar social
adventure.

Many of La Croix du Maine's *auteurs* had good reason to
hide their origins. Ninety out of 378 succeeded well enough so
that we have to stop short of assigning them any official social
status. We may eventually succeed in digging out these un-
speakable verities in the archives. For the moment we must
remain content with identifying 288 of our *auteurs* by social
class. We have 22 unassuming but mostly wealthy bourgeois, 24
gentilhommes whose façade we could not penetrate, 6 actual
noblemen, and 11 men difficult to pin down, of whom 5 were
the sons of university professors and one or two really were
self-made men, including the son of a weaver, an orphan or two
of unknown social origin, and so on. The rest, 222 out of 288
(80 per cent), are *robins*.

La Popelinière's
letter to
Scaliger

Appendix II

This letter, from La Popelinière to Scaliger, is dated January 4, 1604. It was first printed in *Epistres françoises des personnages illustres et doctes à M. Joseph Juste de la Scala, mises en lumière par Jacques de Reves* (Amsterdam, 1624), pp. 303–307. The letter was reprinted by Corrado Vivanti as an appendix to his article "Le scoperte geografiche e gli scritti di Henri de la Popelinière" appearing in *Rivista storica italiana* 74 (1962), pp. 1–25.

Monsieur,

pource que par vos dernieres lettres esquelles me confirmiez
en mes contravis des Sybilles, vous me conseilliez de rendre
l'histoire de particuliere generale sur les plus notables choses tant
humaines que naturelles, j'ay consideré que, pour estre le jugement la plus noble et necessaire partie de l'homme, rien ne le peut
tant solider que le voyage et soigneuse remarque des pays estrangers, afin de nous approcher de la perfection de l'histoire. Si bien
qu'encor que la prattique d'aucuns peuples des Isles et costez
d'Afrique et de l'Amerique m'y aye fort aydé, notamment à
plustost cognoistre et mieux juger de la source, forme, nourriture,
progres et variables effect de toutes les bonnes et mauvaises affec-
tions des hommes, voire de tout ce qu'ont dit, mais en general
seulement, les Philosophes, Historiens et Juris-consultes Grecs
et Romains, soit du droit naturel, soit de celuy des Gens et du
civil de chacun peuple; si est-ce que consideré que comme les
plus signalées actions de tous hommes sont tirées de ces trois
habitudes ou institutions, j'ay creu qu'on ne les pouvoit remarquer
qu'ès peuples civilisez et ceux qu'on appelle assez improprement
sauvages. On a peu de cognoissance de ceux qui le sont au vray.
Si bien, qu'encor que je puisse à peu près juger, tant par ceux
que nous avons descouverts, que par les escrits des aucteurs qui
ont laissé quelque memoire des autres, quelle difference il y a
entre les sauvages et policez, me resteroit neantmoins de voir
les mouvemens et diverses actions des plus anciens et notables
entre les civilisez, qu'on a tousjours estimé estre les Asiens et
d'eux tous les Orientaux, qui comme premiers, à ce que plusieurs
disent, ou du moins, plustost eschaufez par les rayons de ce grand
flambeau, peuvent avoir receu sinon les premiers, certes les plus
vifs, plus nets et continus effects de ces corps celestes, afin de les
rendre plus propres à donner source à tant de belles institutions
humaines; tellement que s'il se falloit estonner ce seroit que
depuis tant de siecles tous jusques icy ont manqué de vouloir ou
de courage, de moyens ou de bonheur pour les aller voir. Notamment depuis cent ans que le chemin y est assez frayé, soit par
terre, soit par mer, le danger semble les y avoir plustost em-
pesché, fors M. Paul Venitien, Loys Vartoman, Am. Vespuce,
Colom Genois et peu d'autres qui nous y ont levé baniere et clair
fanal pour y tenir assez seure route. Mais un seul ne me semble
avoir dressé son voyage à telle fin qui si louable dessein meritoit,
à sçavoir un bien commun puisque les hommes de sauvages et re-

tirez particuliers qu'on les dict avoir esté, se sont peu à peu faicts sociaux et unis par divers liens de police humaine. Car la simple curiosité de voir choses rares semble y avoir poussé les deux premiers, comme le profit et honneur y encouragerent les autres. Aussy ne nous ont ils laissez par leurs escrits que choses legeres et de petit raport pour le particulier de chascun de nous, un seul traict digne d'estre tiré en exemple par aucun estat des nostres.

Il faudroit donques buter à la droicte et entiere cognoissance des hommes, soit au dedans, soit au dehors. Puis de chascun estat et gouvernement d'iceux, en apres de la terre qui les nourrit, de la mer qui leur apporte ses commoditez et fascheries, pour de la monter aux remarques de l'air et du ciel qui peut donner, outre les influences tant rechantées par les Astrologues, certaines marques commodes et avantageuses à la conduite tant de leurs voyages que d'autres desseins qu'ils font de jour en jour.

Vous scavez trop que les plus renommez des Grecs, Solon, Democrite, Empedocle, Pythagore, s'il doit estre dit Grec, Lycurgue, Platon et aultres ne donnerent gueres oultre Babylon, l'Eufrate, ny l'Egypte, d'où neantmoins ils rapporterent la pluspart de ce qu'ils on enschassé en leurs escrits, soit que l'Orient ne fut ouvert aux Grecs que par les conquestes d'Alexandre, soit qu'ils y manquassent de coeur ou de moyens, ou nous de memoire ancienne. Je me persuade qu'un homme judicieux y pourroit remarquer de belles choses s'il avoit les moyens d'y fournir aux frais d'aller, venir acheter, escrire, peindre, graver et se preparer au retour. Democrite y consomma tout son bien, riche qu'il fust au paravant, et en fut moqué à son retour par ses voisins et parens proches, comme Aristote dit qu'on se moquoit des sept sages. Solon fit mieux, promenant fruicts et marchandise de son pays du pris et troque desquelles il fraya aux despens de son sejour et retour en Grece. Ce Prince grec y devroit estre imité. C'est pourquoy, fasché qu'aucun de nostre temps n'entreprend si hault affaire, je vous communique mon desir d'y aller pour l'effectuer, si et comme vous le trouverez bon. J'entens, s'il y a moyen de s'accommoder avec vos Hollandois, qu'on dict y aller d'an en an et environ ce temps. Joinct qu'il m'est incroyable que vous n'ayez bonne cognoissance avec eux, et moins encor que vous ne la voulussiez departir en faveur des lettres à vos amys et mesmes que Messieurs de Leyden n'y fissent ce que desireriez, prians Messieurs les Estats d'y recevoir quelque homme d'honneur qui leur pourroit servir en ce qu'ils le voudroyent employer.

Ce n'est pour empescher leur commerce et moins pour eschantilloner leur profit, ains pour y trouver un contentement d'esprit. Tous me semblent, ailleurs, si clouez à leur profit, tant geinez de folles ambitions et si perdus de vainement jeunes curiositez, que temps ne fut onques, ce semble, si mal disposé à recognoistre son vray bien et honneur.

Vous me direz qu'il faut patir en ces miseres, se regler à son pie et n'entreprendre trop hault. Je l'advoue et l'ay prattiqué par plus de quarante ans, mais mon dessein ne me semble trop hault pour un gentilhomme, veu qu'il est aisé, profitable et de contentement à un simple marchand. Si je l'execute, je seray le premier trompete de la gloire de ceux qui m'y auront assisté. Si non, je me consoleray d'un bon desir et louable essay de faire ce qu'aultre n'a voulu entreprendre. Outre le contentement de tesmoigner à la posterité que ce siecle, bien que vilement conditionné, n'est si sterile de gens d'honneur et de courage que nos nepveus et les estrangers mesme pourroyent penser. Au moins on le verra plus second et mieulx fourny d'outils et instrumens propres à faire belles choses que d'artisans dignes de les concevoir ny conduir à perfection.

J'en attends toutefois vostre avis par le premier, qui me sera pour toute resolution. Au sur plus et sur telle expectative, je prie Dieu, Monsieur, vous maintenir en ses graces et moy ès vostres, d'aussi bon coeur que je desire demeurer à jamais vostre bien humble et affectionné serviteur

                                                            POPELLINIERE

De Paris, ce 4 Janvier 1604

Joan of Arc:
the historiographical
dossier

Appendix III

The historical Joan of Arc, as we know her today, owes much to the zeal of the romantic and nationalist historians of the last century, but, in the last resort, she owes her historical life to the remarkable records of her trials. Without these, she would have remained the half-legendary, shadowy figure of the chroniclers and poets of the Old Régime. It is generally assumed that before Quicherat's publication of the trial records in the 1840s, Joan of Arc was treated as a legendary figure by the historians. There is considerable truth to this view, but the historiographical dossier is more complicated and more interesting than that.

Here I should like to draw a brief sketch of the sixteenth-century portion of this dossier in order to establish some basic points.[1] Among these, the chief one is the question of whether the records of the trial were used by historians before the nineteenth century. The answer is yes. Not only Pasquier used them, but others among his contemporaries as well. The records, it seems clear, have remained available to some degree ever since the fifteenth century, although few historians used them. The question therefore is why historians refused to use this evidence and preferred their own fictions.

If one begins tracing the historical treatment of the *pucelle d'Orléans* from the late fifteenth century on in "the most respected and authoritative histories," one finds first of all that the *pucelle* is characteristically ignored by the historians.

Gilles gives us the story of Joan's arrival at court, of the victory at Orléans, and of the coronation at Reims. He does this in the fewest possible words. Joan herself does not have an important part in the drama whose protagonist, after all, is the king himself. When the annalist reaches the moment of Joan's capture, he concludes her story once and for all with the simple statement that the English "took her to Rouen where they treated her cruelly, executed her and burned her in public." Gilles does not mention the trials for heresy and witchcraft, and he does not mention miracles. He does not want to present her

---

[1] For a brief historiographical survey see Régine Pernoud, *Joan of Arc* (London, 1961), which is not without errors and omissions. More specialized studies exist and they, too, must be used with caution. The best of these is Hanhart's *Das Bild der Jeanne d'Arc*. This book, despite its title, does not go beyond 1600 and is very sketchy for the sixteenth century. Egide Jeanné's *L'image de la pucelle d'Orléans dans la littérature historique française depuis Voltaire* (Paris, 1935) deals mostly with the nineteenth century and is not a work of the highest order. C. W. Lightbody's *The Judgments of Joan* (Cambridge, Mass., 1961) is a careful monograph which does not go beyond 1456.

either as a sorceress or as a saint. She is an embarrassment to him and he will not let her get in the way of his story which concerns the triumph of the king.[2]

Gaguin takes more or less the same position. He tells the story of her arrival and stresses her youth and purity, in defense against the Anglo-Burgundian accusations which made the girl ten years older and denied her virginity. Gaguin is more clearly a sympathizer of Joan's than Gilles was. He also admits —as Gilles did not—that there were uncomfortable implications in this story. The English, he explains, "treated her cruelly because of their hatred of the French and because she dressed like a man." He comments on the trial itself: ". . . before giving sentence, the English had her interrogated—in front of various judges and on a number of separate occasions—on several matters of faith, for they believed that Charles had been helped by this woman instructed in the arts of magic and that he had thus erred in his Catholic faith and for this reason was unworthy of holding his kingdom."[3]

Here we have, then, stated before 1500, the chief difficulty of the royal historians: Joan cannot be anything but a good girl, or Charles owes his kingdom to evil forces. Nor can Joan be too powerful a heroine, for fear of overshadowing the king's own accomplishments. The sources, however, the scraps of anecdotes here and there in the chronicles, presented Joan either as a sorceress or a champion of God. No wonder writers like Gilles and Gaguin prefer to let sleeping dogs lie; the less said, the better.

Emilio is the most skilled practitioner of this "silent version." "As if, in those days, God and mankind together had decided to aid the French," writes the skeptical Italian, "a young girl from Lorraine, about 18 years old, was brought to France." The hero of Emilio's version is the king. Charles *allows* Joan

---

[2] Gilles, *Annales* (Paris, 1553), II, f. lxxix.

[3] Gaguin, *La mer des croniques*, f. 150v–151r, f. 154v.

to help him in battle. Joan herself is not referred to directly after the story of her arrival at court is told. Later her capture is described in a short paragraph as a purely political event; the English burned her, "being both accusers and judges at her trial and no one in this town which they held dared speak up in her defense."[4]

This is the official position of the French state, then, in the sixteenth century. The king's historians are sympathetic to Joan to the extent that they give no credence to the English and Burgundian accusations against her. They do not dwell upon the great trial at Rouen; perhaps this is distasteful to them. In any case they do not seem to think it necessary to defend Joan against her accusers. Strangely, they ignore the rehabilitation trial entirely, and yet this trial is the only conceivable source for thinking well of Joan. It was at this trial that she was exonerated, here that friendly witnesses spoke for her and denounced her previous judges. Emilio prefers to pass things over in silence. The important thing was to lay old ghosts, to ensure that Joan figured neither as saint nor as sorceress in the wings of the royal drama. Perhaps the kings and their historians at the turn of the century were hoping that the whole story would eventually drop out of the chronicles and be forgotten in time.

There were, however, important questions: if the *pucelle* was neither saint nor sorceress, if she was merely an ordinary farm girl, how was she able to command armies and inspire passionate loyalty and zeal among her followers? What prompted the king's decision in the first place to place her in a position of command? These difficulties led straight to the rationalist version, "a rumor which has run straight from the mouths of those who lived in those times to the ears of the men of our time," a rumor to the effect that the whole affair was devised

---

[4] Paul Eemyle, *Histoire des faicts, gestes, . . .* , trans. Jean Renart (Paris, 1598), p. 621.

by clever courtiers and generals.[5] Du Haillan gives the best
summary of the rationalist version, and he thinks it is a plausible one:

> While the English roamed the countryside at will, the King
> would not budge from Meun where he was busy making love to
> his *belle Agnès* and building gardens on his estate. The King did
> not understand the gravity of his own situation nor that of his
> kingdom, and this added even further to the misery of France.
> But God, who kept a merciful eye on our country, caused Jean
> Bastard of Orléans, Poton de Xaintraille, La Hire and other
> valiant knights to be born just in time: these men saved France,
> making up for the King's imbecility through their courage and
> virtue.
> Here then are the English in front of Orléans, laying siege to
> it: here the King's majesty and his name are held in contempt,
> because of his weakness and his misfortunes. At this point, these
> three knights raised France and her King out of their ruin by
> means of a miracle of religion—either a genuine miracle or a
> simulated one.
> There was a young girl of twenty-two from Vaucouleurs in
> Lorraine named Joan, raised in the fields with the sheep, who
> was brought to the King and told him that she came inspired by
> God to promise him that she would run the English out of France.
> The miracle of this girl—whether it was a genuine miracle or
> not—raised the hearts of the lords, of the people, and of the
> King, all of whom had lost heart; such is the power of religion,
> and, often, of superstition. For there are some who say that this
> Joan was the mistress of Jean Bastard of Orléans, others say she
> was Baudricourt's wench and others still that she belonged to
> Poton.

The rationalist explanation, as summed up by Du Haillan,
runs like this: the war chiefs "decided to create a miracle, which
is the thing in the world most likely to revive the spirits and lift
the hearts of men, especially the simple-minded; and then, the

---

[5] "Toutefois il a depuis couru un bruit, qui des bouches de ceux qui vivaient
de ce temps là ont coulé dedans les bouches et oreilles des hommes de nostre
temps, que ce miracle de cette fille était supposé et apposté." Du Haillan,
Histoire generale des roys de France, II, p. 955.

time was propitious for such superstitions, the people being very devout, superstitious, and ruined."

"Some have found it ill-advised," Du Haillan admits, "that I should tell all this and thus deprive our Frenchmen of an opinion they have so long held of a saintly happening and miracle." But, he explains, "I wanted to tell this because time—which uncovers all things—has uncovered it. And then, anyhow, this is not so important a matter that it has to be believed as an article of faith."[6]

This was an important matter, and neither Emilio's discretion nor Du Haillan's debunking could do away with the embarrassments of the affair. Nicolas Vignier's *Sommaire de l'histoire des françois*, published very shortly after Du Haillan's *Estat et succez*, reflects all the confusions and embarrassments the story of Joan of Arc could cause an official court historian in the 1570s. Vignier is very much aware of the hostile English and Burgundian versions. He is also aware of the rationalist version. Like his official predecessors, he tries to play the story down, but he is not entirely successful. More than Emilio ever had, Vignier feels the need to defend Joan's reputation. He knows of the trial records, and his Protestantism does not readily allow for saints and miracles in these latter days.

He is dutiful; he is cautious; he is erudite; and he cannot come to any conclusion. Dutifully, he tells the story of her arrival at court, here following Emilio, Gaguin, Gilles, and the others. Cautiously, he writes that Joan "claims to be inspired and sent by God." Discreetly, he pictures her part in the military campaigns as secondary, but he cannot help observing that "the affairs of France set themselves right so suddenly, that it seemed as if God wanted to set things straight again by means of that girl." Not that this simple peasant girl could really have swung the balance—the king, of course, and his lieutenants must receive credit for the victories. Nevertheless, from the

---

[6] Bernard de Gerard Du Haillan, *De l'estat et succez des affaires de France* (Paris, 1580), p. 124a.

time of Joan's arrival to the moment of her capture "there were very few memorable enterprises and exploits of war undertaken by the French at the planning and execution of which she was not present." The girl, in some unfathomable way, must have brought luck to the French.

What of the English case? Vignier is a critical scholar who will not let himself be blinded by political partisanship. Could the English have a case? "Even if she had been as the English made her out to be at her death," he argues judiciously, how much does that explain? If one believes that she was a *putain* and a heretic, this still does not explain how "a young girl trained only to guard sheep could suddenly, in an instant, become adept at handling weapons and horses and should lead men in war."

If the English version is implausible, what about Du Haillan's story? Is it more plausible that "there has been more ruse and imposture or superstition than miracle or truth in this affair?" No, Vignier feels "obliged to reject this opinion under the weight of too many arguments and too much weighty testimony."

The testimony in question is the record of the trial "which can still be seen in the hands of several people." Vignier may not have had the opportunity to study the records very carefully. He may have given them a quick reading or, more likely, he may have received a thorough report from someone like Pasquier. What he knows of the trial is enough to make him think that "the replies and confessions she made in answer to the judges' questions, which are written down in the records, show —even if one takes them at their worst—more superstition than wickedness on her part."

Vignier cannot make up his mind. He cannot believe that Joan was acting a part: "It is impossible that a whore could have played the part this Joan played in front of a king for so long and in full evidence of the entire court." If she was not playing a part, where did her power come from? Was she a saint or a sorceress after all?—an impossible conclusion. The

English taunts embarrass him: they say that "it was ignominious for the King of France to have re-established his kingdom
with her help." To this Vignier can only answer that it was
surely even more ignominious for the English to have been
defeated by her. In the end Vignier takes the modest defensive
position that he sees no reason why the French should be
ashamed of the episode, even if it were true that Joan did falsely
boast of having been sent by God. For, although all lies are
odious in the eyes of God, those lies made for the salvation
and deliverance of one's country have always seemed to the
judgment of men to merit praise rather than punishment.[7]

In 1579, then, the royal historiographer Vignier finds it necessary to reassure his countrymen: they need not feel ashamed
of Joan of Arc. No matter who the girl was, even if she committed sins or crimes, what she did was for the greater glory
of France and therefore excusable. Among serious people the
story of Joan was an embarrassment. There is not a trace yet
of the grandiose national legend which will be so dear to the
nineteenth-century historians. Joan is far from being made a
saint; for this she will have to wait until the twentieth century.
Even her name does not yet have that noble ring to it: she is
simply Jeanne, daughter of Jacques Darc, *laboureur*. Later
historians will call her Jeanne d'Arc; the simple apostrophe
seems to make the name more suitable for the heroine of a
chivalric epic.

The question which necessarily confronts us is this: what
forces were at work to make a national heroine of Joan?
Granted that the full proportions of her triumph in the French
national consciousness did not manifest themselves until after
the French Revolution, when all the other heroes of the French
past had become unacceptable because they were not members
of the Third Estate, nevertheless, the history of her popularity
does not begin in 1789. If I were asked to assign a date to the
beginning of her popularity, I would choose 1579.

[7] Vignier, *Sommaire*, pp. 369ff.

In some ways, to be sure, her popularity had never ceased since she fought at the siege of Orléans; there was the local memory of her in Orléans, there was her presence in poetry and religious literature, and there was, always, her incalculable presence in the popular mind. Oral tradition and folk memory could have died out in time, though. Joan might well have become nothing more than a fairy-tale heroine, collected by some Perrault or Grimm, eventually a presence in nursery rhymes, a witch in Burgundy perhaps, a princess in Anjou.

She was saved from this fate for two reasons: first, there were the trial records; second, her story was inextricably tied to the story of the kingdom of France. This is why Vignier cannot simply pass her under silence. Somehow or other Joan played an important part in the salvation of the kingdom. Whether she was a mysterious outside agent descending upon the scene or whether she was a successful propaganda device of Charles' court—one way or the other, her actions and the honor of the French crown are inseparable. The kingdom cannot owe its sudden change of fortune either to a sorceress or to a slut.

That the dauphin Charles should have changed, that this timid "imbecile" should suddenly have turned into a great statesman, was almost impossible to conceive, given the psychology of a sixteenth-century historian. The intervention of the farm girl from Lorraine had been adduced as the only possible explanation of Charles' sudden recovery by the fifteenth-century chroniclers. Their successors agreed in this; they had to. The erudite Pasquier is almost alone in attributing the sudden triumphs of the French to the dynastic difficulties of the English, among other causes. For the most part, historical explanation remains in the grip of ancient and medieval views of character and causation. The *pucelle* was useful to the historians: she was the cause of Charles' victory. Therefore, she had to be an honorable girl. Furthermore, the trial records confirmed this view; despite their evident malice, the judges found her guilty of no immoral conduct.

That one could not simply dismiss the story, for all these reasons, is clear from Vignier's attitude. In 1579 one could not even sidestep the issues as Gilles or Emilio once did—not if one took one's work seriously, not if one knew the trial records. More so than Vignier, Belleforest demonstrates this very clearly. His *Annals* were published in the same year. Here, for the first time to the best of my knowledge, the trial records are quoted at great length. Belleforest is immersed in these documents. He has the annals of his predecessors in front of him. He has studied Gilles, but he cannot content himself with Gilles' terse notations. It is not so much the military victories and the events at court which interest him here. Without hesitation he goes directly to that part of Joan's story which the earlier chroniclers had ignored entirely: the trial at Rouen and the rehabilitation trial twenty years later.

Obviously Belleforest's motives are different from those of Gilles or Emilio. He is not merely narrating the *gestes* of the kings of France. He is, instead, writing the "universal history of France," as he puts it. In this perspective Joan's trial and her reputation are much more important than the events of the siege at Orléans. Belleforest explains why this is so, very candidly: ". . . for it would be a great dishonour for our kings if a mad girl—a sorceress and a voluptuary, the plaything of soldiers—were at the same time she to whom France owed so much that she must be confessed to be the deliverer of our fathers from the English captivity and she who returned the crown to the legitimate hands of the French dynasty that had lost it."

There we have it. There is no getting away from it. "If the *pucelle* had been a witch, there is no question but that the King himself would have to be considered an accomplice to her crime."[8] Belleforest has to defend Joan's honor. He admits freely that he is all the more "emotionally involved in this cause

8 ". . . car si la Pucelle eust esté sorcière, c'est sans faillir que le Roy eust esté coulpable de son crime." Belleforest, *Les grandes annales,* p. 1174.

because he sees others sticking to the false opinion that Joan was justly burned by the English and that far from being a girl and a virgin, she was a wench who profited from her beauty and prostituted herself impudently."[9]

Partisan he is, but he cites his sources "so that one cannot accuse him of depending on mere reasoning and plausible arguments." He does have the sources, almost all those available to us in the twentieth century. Mostly he depends on the records of the two trials. He seems to have had access to these through the generosity of the monks of St. Victor, whose help he acknowledges. On the other hand, he may have been working from extracts and copies, but those must have been adequate because he gives literal translations and accurate paraphrases of the articles of the Promoter against the accused at the Rouen trial and many other pieces of documentation.[10]

In Belleforest's *Annals* the modern Joan is born. Rescued from oblivion, she plays an important part in the "histoire universelle de France." She is innocent and straightforward: her voice is that of the accused Johanna of the Rouen trial. It is an authentic voice. The judges, "ces Rabins qui faisoyent des sçavãts à l'endroit d'une bergère," are the creatures of the English masters who want her dead. She is "excommunicated, declared heretic and handed over to the secular arm to appease the rage of her enemies: otherwise the English lords threatened to have the doctors killed." Belleforest argues against the Promoter's accusations point by point. He makes a good case for the defense. As he sees it, she is a national martyr.

He apologizes for having spent so much time discussing this historical problem. He wishes it understood that he does

[9] "Et de tant plus m'affectionne ie à ceste cause que ie voy plusieurs aheurtez à ceste faulse opinion que de dire que iustement Jeanne fust bruslée par les Anglois & que tant s'en faut qu'elle fut pucelle & vierge que plustost elle estoit une garse faisant profit de sa beaute & se prostituant come impudique." *Ibid.*, p. 1092.

[10] *Ibid.*, pp. 1093bff., is a paraphrase of the *processus ordinarius*. For the original text see *Procés de condamnation de Jeanne d'Arc,* ed. Pierre Tisset (Société de l'Histoire de France, Paris, 1960), I, pp. 192ff.

not dwell on the *pucelle*'s story "pour en bastir quelque superstition." He is not making a saint out of her, only a national heroine. His aim is to "revenger la France."[11]

The same motives, the same position, and the same documentation are to be found in Pasquier's *Recherches*. I would suppose that Pasquier worked with the trial records even before Belleforest did, although he withheld publication for a long time. His study is more thorough, more sophisticated, and closer to the text of the documents in front of him. His is much better history, but the point remains the same. The *pucelle*'s reputation must be defended because it is tied to the reputation of the royal family and of the entire nation. This can be done because of the clear evidence of the trial records.

Evidently, others besides Belleforest and Pasquier studied these records, judging from Vignier's remarks. The theologian Richer used them in his unpublished work,[12] and it is unlikely that Pasquier could have kept the records in his study for four years without letting his friends look at them. Still, Belleforest and Pasquier are the only historians I know—before the eighteenth century—who actually cited these documents in their published works. No doubt, we will eventually run into some others, but this will not alter the picture. Before the Revolution, despite the availability of the records, it was exceptional for historians to make use of them.

Belleforest and Pasquier are among the few—perhaps the only ones—who can treat Joan of Arc without lapsing into one of several varieties of fiction: the fiction of the rationalists, the

---

[11] "Au reste ie me suis assez longuement arresté à recueillir ce procez, non pour en bastir quelque superstition, ains seulement pour revenger la France et les Roys d'icelle de vanité & sottise sur eux iectée par ceux qui blasment ceste fille: car ce serait un grand deshonneur à noz Roys si une garse folle, sorcière & addonnée à tous plaisirs & servant de jouet aux soldats, eust esté celle à qui la France soit si redevable que de la confesser pour celle qui delivra noz peres de la capitivité Angloise & qui reunit la couronne ès mains de sang legitime de France à qui on l'avoit osté." Belleforest, *Les grandes annales,* p. 1100b.

[12] See Hanhart, *Das Bild der Jeanne d'Arc,* p. 101.

fiction of the devout, or the fiction of those who pretend that her story is of no importance. All three of these varieties flourished from the start and continued to flourish until the end of the Old Régime, and not for lack of historical evidence to the contrary.

I can think of no better way to illustrate this point than to refer the reader to Mézeray's account.[13] Mézeray knows very well what the trial records show. He had read them in Belleforest or Pasquier, but this evidence is entirely irrelevant as far as he is concerned. To be sure, "her trial can be found in full detail in our authors." He points out that Joan was interrogated on some sixty or eighty points "with all the subtlety of the finest scholastic method." Her replies to these interrogations, he writes, "are so pertinent, so humble and so Christian that they indict her judges."[14]

All very well, but Mézeray is not interested in the trial. His talent can operate more freely when unhampered by documentary evidence. His story begins with Charles, the same Charles whom we may remember as the imbecile fondling his *belle Agnès* in Du Haillan's account. Nothing so sacrilegious in Mézeray—Charles precipitates divine intervention by ordering processions and fasts in all his lands. Moved by deep piety, he frequently enters his chapel, throws himself face down on the ground, and bathed in tears, he implores his immediate superior, God, to show him a sign.

Mézeray, like so many seventeenth-century historians, is privy to the innermost thoughts of the Almighty himself. He explains that the Heavenly Father, moved by the humbled and prostrate countenance of the dauphin, decides to help him and devises a way of doing it. To make sure that everyone would clearly perceive where this help came from and know that all

---

[13] Mézeray, *Histoire de France* (Paris, 1646), II, pp. 11ff.

[14] ". . . son Procés se trouve tout au long dans nos Autheurs"; "Il y a des interrogations sur 60 ou 80 articles"; "Et neanmoins ses responces sont si pertinentes, si humbles & si chrestiennes, qu'elles font le procés à ceux qui l'ont condamnée." *Ibid.*, p. 17.

strength and wisdom come only from Him—for God behaves suspiciously like the king of France in these courtiers' histories—He chooses a poor and ignorant shepherdess as His instrument.

In Mézeray's story this simple shepherdess[15] looms large. Leaving a trail of miracles, she does actually lead the king to victory, but it is understood all along that she is not personally important—she is merely a tool of divine providence. Joan's capture is explained by the fact that she had exceeded her mission: she should have gone home after the coronation.[16] But she stayed on, and God, "who insists on being obeyed punctually, no longer felt obliged to continue his miracles in her favor."

Mézeray's epic story ends with a dramatic flourish precisely where, in the theater, it ought to end: at the stake. And if there does not happen to be any testimony for this event, Mézeray has no qualms about inventing the action. The choicest part of it, to my mind, is Joan's speech at the stake. "Well, have you got what you wanted?" she addresses her torturers. "Have you at last brought me to a place where you no longer need fear me? Cowards that you are, you are frightened of a girl and, too weak to be soldiers, you have become executioners! Impious and abominable creatures, you struggle in vain against God. Tell me, do you really expect to change the decrees of the Almighty through your tyranny?" At last Joan dies and a white dove emerges out of the flames. The victim's heart turns out to be fireproof.

Piety and chivalry, the courtly and the miraculous, are mixed in the right proportions to reduce Mézeray's readers to tears. Throughout, he never loses sight of the chief point, which is the special character of the French monarchy, the special protection it enjoys from above. Those decrees Joan is warning

---

[15] Belleforest knew better: her parents were of "moyenne fortune" according to him.

[16] This is a common explanation in the older chronicles.

the English about have to do, naturally, with the eventual and inevitable triumph and greatness of the French monarchy.

That Mézeray should choose to replace the painstaking historical researches of Belleforest and Pasquier with dramatic fictions is no surprise. If there is anything surprising about Mézeray, it is rather that he should make such a fuss over the *pucelle*: such an effusion of patriotism and religious sentiment! In this, as in so much else, Mézeray remains closer to the historians of an earlier generation than to his contemporaries.[17] His enthusiasm is already misplaced in the *grand siècle*. The normal thing from now on will be to ignore the affair once again or to chronicle it in the fewest possible words.[18]

Both the "silent" and the rationalist versions are commonly found in the course of the seventeenth and eighteenth centuries. The erudite version pioneered by Belleforest and Pasquier does not seem to find any followers. This could not be the product of ignorance: new editions of Pasquier's *Recherches* continued to be published into the eighteenth century. I suspect that if one looked hard enough, one would find the historical Joan of Arc and a knowledge of the trials in the obscure circles of scholars in this period. This would not change the fundamental fact that some profound cultural change occurred in the early seventeenth century. The patriotism of the 1570s disappears, and with it that understanding of Joan of Arc which would not be revived until the nineteenth century. Until then, Joan remains a pious legend to the devout, a scandal to the skeptics, and an embarrassment to the official historians.

[17] See W. H. Evans, *L'historien Mézeray* (Paris, 1930).

[18] Jeanné, *L'image de la pucelle*, p. 1.

Index

213

Assistant professor of history at the University of Illinois, Chicago Circle Campus, GEORGE HUPPERT received his M.A. from the University of Wisconsin and his PH.D. from the University of California, Berkeley. He was a Woodrow Wilson Fellow in 1958–59, a Social Science Research Council Fellow in 1961–62, and an American Council of Learned Societies Fellow in 1965–66. THE IDEA OF PERFECT HISTORY is Mr. Huppert's first book.

University of Illinois Press